About RUSI

The Royal United Services Institute (RUSI) is an independent think tank engaged in cutting-edge defence and security research. A unique institution, founded in 1831 by the Duke of Wellington, RUSI embodies nearly two centuries of forward thinking, free discussion and careful reflection on defence and security matters.

RUSI consistently brings to the fore vital policy issues to both domestic and global audiences, enhancing its growing reputation as a 'thought-leader institute', winning the Prospect Magazine Think Tank of the Year Award 2008 and Foreign Policy Think Tank of the Year Award 2009. RUSI is a British institution, but operates with an international perspective. Satellite offices in Doha and Washington, DC reinforce its global reach. It has amassed over the years an outstanding reputation for quality and objectivity. Its heritage and location at the heart of Whitehall, together with a range of contacts both inside and outside government, give RUSI a unique insight and authority.

RUSI is a registered charity (no. 210639)
ISBN 0-85516-153-1

Published on behalf of The Royal United Services Institute for Defence and Security Studies by Routledge Journals an imprint of Taylor & Francis, 4 Park Square, Milton Park, Abingdon OX14 4RN, UK

T0347278

About Whitehall Papers

The *Whitehall Paper* series provides in-depth studies of specific developments, issues or themes in the field of national and international defence and security. Published occasionally throughout the year, *Whitehall Papers* reflect the highest standards of original research and analysis, and are invaluable background material for specialists and policy-makers alike.

Subscriptions

Please send subscription orders to: USA/Canada: Taylor & Francis Inc., Journals Department, 325 Chestnut Street, 8th Floor, Philadelphia, PA 19106, USA. UK/Rest of World: Routledge Journals, T&F Customer Services, T&F Informa UK Ltd, Sheepen Place, Colchester, Essex, CO3 3LP, UK.

The Global Partnership Against WMD
Success and Shortcomings of G8 Threat Reduction since 9/11

Alan Heyes, Wyn Q Bowen and Hugh Chalmers

www.rusi.org

Royal United Services Institute for Defence and Security Studies

The Global Partnership Against WMD: Success and Shortcomings of G8 Threat Reduction since 9/11
By Alan Heyes, Wyn Q Bowen and Hugh Chalmers
First published 2011

Whitehall Papers series

Series Editor: Professor Malcolm Chalmers
Editors: Adrian Johnson and Ashlee Godwin
Editorial Assistant: Dave Jackson

RUSI is a registered charity (no. 210639)
ISBN 0855161531

Published on behalf of the Royal United Services Institute
for Defence and Security Studies
by
Routledge Journals, an imprint of Taylor & Francis, 4 Park Square, Milton Park,
Abingdon OX14 4RN

SUBSCRIPTIONS
Please send subscription orders to:

USA/Canada: Taylor & Francis Inc., Journals Department, 325 Chestnut Street,
8th Floor, Philadelphia, PA 19106 USA

UK/Rest of World: Routledge Journals, T&F Customer Services, T&F Informa UK Ltd,
Sheepen Place, Colchester, Essex, CO3 3LP, UK

Contents

I. INTRODUCTION

The 9/11 terrorist attacks prompted a new urgency in efforts to deal with chemical, biological, radiological and nuclear (CBRN) proliferation. In Washington and elsewhere, the potential acquisition and use by terrorist groups of CBRN materials and weapons subsequently came to be perceived as a much increased threat. The Bush administration moved quickly to respond to the unprecedented events – and to the resultant impact on international threat perceptions related to CBRN terrorism – by seeking the commitment of its fellow G8 governments to establish a new initiative through which to collaborate on threat reduction, and to jointly commit a substantial amount of funding and technical expertise to implement projects in line with an agreed set of priorities. The new initiative was launched in 2002 at the G8 summit in Kananaskis, Alberta, Canada.[1] It was a clear policy signal on the part of the Bush administration that the United States could not address the challenge by itself within a politically acceptable timescale, and that other countries needed to contribute to threat reduction work in a more focused and significant way.

In particular, the 'Global Partnership (GP) Against the Spread of Weapons and Materials of Mass Destruction'

---

[1] Annex A includes the key GP documents from the summit. See also 'The G8 Global Partnership Against the Spread of Weapons and Materials of Mass Destruction', Statement by the Group of Eight Leaders, Kananaskis, Canada, 27 June 2002, <http://www.canadainternational.gc.ca/g8/summit-sommet/2002/global_partnership-partenariat_mondial.aspx?lang=eng>, accessed 17 June 2011.

subsequently encouraged some twenty-two[2] countries and the European Union to pledge up to $20 billion to address the CBRN legacy challenge in the period up to 2012; half of the initial funding ($10 billion) was to come from the United States under its existing $1 billion per annum Cooperative Threat Reduction (CTR) programmes, with the remaining $10 billion to be provided by other G8 countries along with further contributions from countries that joined the GP after the summit. By 2010, an additional $375 million had been committed or spent by these non-G8 countries on GP-related projects (see Annex F for a breakdown of funding by non-G8 countries). The creation of the GP constituted the first time that so many countries had agreed to collaborate on a range of non-proliferation, security and nuclear safety programmes as well as to commit such an unprecedented amount of resources to implementing them, in terms of both funding and technical assistance.

The ten-year duration of the GP was an explicit acknowledgement that many threat reduction projects would take time to deliver, given the requirement to build new infrastructure or to enhance security culture and practices in particular countries. The G8 leaders agreed that the GP's initial priorities, in terms of projects and spending, lay in Russia because it possessed what was by far the largest inventory of weapons and materials. The key priorities of the GP were agreed collectively in 2002 and embraced: the dismantlement of some 190 of Russia's decommissioned nuclear submarines; the destruction of around 4 million chemical munitions, many containing nerve agents; the redirection of former weapons scientists; and the disposal of fissile materials.

---

[2] Countries and organisations that have contributed funding to GP projects since 2002 include: Australia, Belgium, Canada, the Czech Republic, Denmark, Finland, France, Germany, Ireland, Italy, Japan, the Netherlands, New Zealand, Norway, Poland, the Republic of Korea, the Russian Federation, Sweden, Switzerland, Ukraine, the United Kingdom and the United States. The European Union and the Nuclear Threat Initiative, a US NGO, have also contributed funding to GP projects. Kazakhstan has joined the GP as a recipient country.

The Study

After some nine years in operation and the implementation of multiple separate threat reduction projects by GP countries, international policy-makers recently agreed, during the French G8 summit at Deauville in May 2011, to extend the initiative beyond the initially agreed period, which was set to expire in 2012. It is in this context that this Whitehall Paper evaluates the performance of the GP to date. The research was made possible by a generous grant from the John D and Catherine T MacArthur Foundation to examine international threat reduction efforts under the GP and to generate new knowledge and understanding of European policies and practices therein.[3]

The paper is informed by research interviews with dozens of officials with responsibility for the GP and other CBRN mitigation-related activities from thirteen governments (including all the G8 countries), the European Commission, the European Bank for Reconstruction and Development (EBRD) and the International Atomic Energy Agency (IAEA), along with a number of project contractors and non-governmental organisations. A number of interviews were conducted with officials from countries in which GP-related projects have been planned or implemented. Annex B includes a list of the organisations whose officials contributed to the research process on a non-attributable basis.[4] The interviews were based around a standardised set of questions related to the evolution and implementation of the GP from 2002 to 2010, and the potential future direction of multilateral threat reduction. The paper also draws on primary source documentation related to the G8 and GP. The study is largely reliant on primary source materials, given

---

[3] An initial summary of the findings of this project was published in the *Bulletin of the Atomic Scientists*. See Alan J Heyes and Wyn Q Bowen, 'Silent partnership: The G-8's nonproliferation program', *Bulletin of the Atomic Scientists* (Vol. 66, No. 2, March–April 2010), pp.17–26.

[4] Citations of specific interview material in the footnotes only provide a code letter and a date.

the paucity of detailed and relevant analyses in the existing secondary literature in this area.[5]

The study is divided into four chapters. Chapter II briefly examines the evolution of the G8 as a non-proliferation actor and the context within which the GP was established in 2001–02. It demonstrates that the events of 9/11 in combination with the high-level political buy-in of the G8 leaders made possible the extraordinary commitment of resources to CBRN threat reduction in June 2002. It highlights why the GP approach was chosen and why it is different to some of the formal approaches that went before and which were associated with other international bodies such as the IAEA.

Chapter III examines the GP at a programmatic level. It shows that the GP has realised some significant achievements since 2002 in the context of chemical weapons destruction and submarine dismantlement in Russia. However, it is argued that these Russian priorities have been pursued at the expense of more pressing CBRN challenges such as enhancing the security of nuclear, radiological and biological material and the related knowledge possessed by scientists and technicians, both within the former Soviet Union (FSU) and elsewhere. It is shown that the consensus nature of the GP decision-making process, and Russia's refusal to sanction a more global and targeted initiative, were pivotal in preventing the GP from adopting an approach that would have more effectively addressed challenges of greater direct relevance to the prevention of CBRN terrorism. The chapter also highlights further weaknesses, including the failure of some G8 countries to deliver on their initial funding pledges, and the inability of the GP Working Group to provide strategic guidance and to

---

[5] One exception, for example, is Ian Anthony's *Reducing Threats at the Source: A European Perspective on Cooperative Threat Reduction* (Oxford: Oxford University Press, 2004), p. 136. However, this SIPRI Research Report was written at the very outset of the GP before it was possible to conduct an in-depth examination of its achievements and shortcomings.

conduct effective evaluations and discussions of evolving priorities and implementation.

Chapter IV examines the operation of the GP at the working level. In contrast to the macro-level problems discussed in the previous chapter, it is argued that the GP has been much more effective at this practical level. The chapter examines the notable achievements in this respect, including: the establishment of a strong network of officials and technical experts drawn from across the GP community of states and organisations responsible for implementing threat reduction programmes; the development of trust and good working relations between FSU and GP donor countries at the working level; and the sharing of best practice related to project management and risk assessment. In addition to the positive story at the working level, the chapter also argues that the GP has resulted in some unforeseen spin-off benefits that have been highly beneficial for some of the partner countries.

The final chapter examines the core challenges and issues that the recently renewed GP multilateral threat reduction programme will need to address if the initiative is to remain relevant beyond 2012 and aligned with the current and evolving global CBRN security environment. These challenges include reforming the role of the GP Working Group and moving the GP beyond the G8 context in order to engage key countries such as China and India. The development of a framework better suited to providing a regional oversight approach to multilateral threat reduction is also addressed, as is the need to reform the Working Group to make it more responsive and strategically oriented. The importance of completing ongoing GP projects in Russia and the wider FSU is also highlighted.

A series of case studies of GP projects are included in Annex C to demonstrate the impact of some of the major projects in terms of meeting key GP objectives. The case studies are designed to support the analysis in the main text by providing additional details of some of the challenges confronted in specific areas and the solutions developed in the context of the GP.

Box 1: Key Achievements of the Global Partnership

- Long-term funding pledge provided greater stability to implement complex projects with a long timescale for completion
- Flexible agreement allowed funding from a wide range of donors through a range of instruments
- Strong political support has opened doors in countries formerly very secretive and suspicious of international interest in their CBRN work
- Increased transparency and openness of countries' CBRN-related activities
- Destruction of a significant proportion of Russia's chemical weapons (some 20,000 tonnes)
- Dismantlement of almost all of Russia's decommissioned submarines (some 190)
- Ensured the cessation of the production of weapons-grade plutonium in Russia
- Significant enhancement of nuclear safety in FSU states
- A framework that enabled more effective collaboration and co-operation between states and international agencies such as the IAEA
- A structure to allow for the efficient sharing of lessons learned and best practices in CBRN risk mitigation
- Enabled the GP community to acquire the expertise and confidence to tackle global threats outside the FSU in equally, if not more, challenging environments
- Started the process of enhancing professional responsibility within CBRN scientific communities and their facilities to secure sensitive expertise
- Reduced the prospect of the nuclear renaissance being compromised by a failure to address nuclear safety.

Box 2: Shortcomings and Missed Opportunities of the Global Partnership

- Too much focus on Russia's priorities of chemical weapons destruction and submarine dismantlement at the expense of other priorities, especially securing fissile and radiological materials
- Full range of CBRN security and proliferation risks identified in 2002 only partially addressed
- Limited focus on bio-security and bio-safety
- Failure to become the hub of international CBRN risk mitigation
- No formal strategy developed to encourage and lobby other countries to participate
- Reliant on consensus to move initiatives forward
- No effective assessment and evaluation process to guide and influence future initiatives and promote lessons learnt.

II. THE G8, NON-PROLIFERATION AND THE GLOBAL PARTNERSHIP

The announcement of the GP came a quarter of a century after the first G7 summit *communiqué* that made a direct reference to nuclear non-proliferation.[1] Similarly, the EU and many of its member states had been actively involved in threat reduction work for some time prior to 2002, albeit at a much lower level than the United States, which played a leadership role during the immediate post-Cold War years of the early 1990s. While there is evidently a pre-2002 history of the G7 and then the G8 member states addressing non-proliferation challenges, the growth in concern about terrorism that followed 9/11, including the potential ease of acquisition of CBRN materials or weaponry in the FSU for use by terrorists in mass casualty attacks, did two significant things. First, through the GP it led to an unprecedented commitment of resources by the G8 to address the non-proliferation problem. Prior to the Kananaskis Summit, the only financial pledges initiated by the G8 were towards a specific budget for a programme of non-proliferation work in relation to the disposition of 34 tonnes of Russian weapons-grade plutonium; even then, not all of the G8 countries contributed,[2]

---

[1] 'Declaration: Downing Street Summit Conference', G7 summit *communiqué*, London, May 1977, <http://www.g8.utoronto.ca/summit/1977london/communique.html>, accessed 17 June 2011.

[2] The US-Russian Plutonium Management and Disposition Agreement (PMDA) of June 2000, and the joint US-Russian statement of intention related to the non-separation of additional weapons-grade plutonium, subsequently led to several G8 countries pledging some $800 million

with Italy and Germany declining to pledge funds. Second, the GP gave the EU and its member states a renewed focus and commitment to invest significant amounts of resources into threat reduction by creating a partnership through which all effectively contributed in terms of both funding and technical resources.

To provide the background to these developments, the current chapter seeks to consider some of the pre-history of the GP and the genesis of the initiative itself. Four main areas are addressed. First, consideration is given to the evolution of the G7/G8 as a non-proliferation actor from the late 1970s through to the 9/11 terrorist attacks. How Europe and the US approached threat reduction prior to 2002 is then examined, before considering how the new security context post-9/11 raised expectations that some non-state actors would seek to harness CBRN capabilities in their quest for perpetrating mass effect attacks. The chapter concludes with an examination of the post-9/11 origins of the GP concept and of the Kananaskis Summit declaration.

1975: The G7 and the 'Rambouillet Effect'

The leaders of the United States, Japan, Germany, France, Britain, Italy and Canada gathered for their first multilateral meeting as the G7 in 1975 at Rambouillet, France. The focus was on managing global economic performance, a core priority that has remained in place at all subsequent G7 and G8 summits.

---

towards this programme at the 2000 G8 summit in Okinawa, following which these commitments (by the US, Canada, France, the UK and Japan) were rolled into their GP pledges at Kananaskis. In April 2010, the PMDA was renewed by the US and Russia and Moscow's future implementation of its plutonium disposition will no longer depend on additional American and other sources of funding. Little, if any, of the pledged funding from Canada, France, Japan and the UK has actually been used for plutonium disposition activities, although the 2010 agreement between the US and Russia allows for the original American pledge to be taken up. '2000 Plutonium Management and Disposition Agreement', Fact Sheet, Office of the Spokesman, US State Department, 13 April 2010, <http://www.state. gov/r/pa/prs/ps/2010/04/140097.htm>, accessed 17 June 2011.

Non-proliferation as a security issue was not addressed by the group for another two years until the London Summit of 1977. There it was discussed in the context of the expected expansion of nuclear energy and the stated need of the G7 economies to reduce their dependence on oil, following the oil crisis of 1973–74. Nuclear was identified as an essential source of power that needed to be expanded in scope to fulfil the 'world's energy requirements', while 'reducing the risks of nuclear proliferation' was also recognised as a priority.[3]

Nicholas Bayne writes that, 'Three reasons, each of a different kind, contributed to the genesis of the G7 summits in 1975'. The first reason was the need for 'reconciling interdependence' in a world where the much greater economic interdependence that had developed since the 1950s, along with 'confusion on the monetary scene', the oil crisis in 1973–74 and the subsequent global recession had combined to create 'tension between economic interdependence and national sovereignty, which only heads of government seemed likely to resolve'. Second, as the European countries and Japan were experiencing faster economic growth than the United States at this point, the international economic leadership role played by America since the 1950s evidently needed supplementing with greater leadership and management contributions from these other economically developed states. The third reason involved the preference of Western political leaders of the day for smaller, select, more informal and more personal meetings to discuss issues of direct relevance to their countries.[4] Directly related to this reasoning, Bayne notes that there was a conviction on the part of these leaders that 'heads of government could bring a unique and essential contribution beyond the capacities of officials and other ministers'. This encompassed several dimensions. To begin with, 'heads of government could integrate policies normally treated separately by ministers or departments with specific responsibilities. They were also best placed to reconcile the various demands of foreign policy and domestic

---

?[3] 'Declaration: Downing Street Summit Conference', *op. cit.*

[4] Nicholas Bayne, *Hanging In There: The G7 and G8 Summit in Maturity and Renewal* (Aldershot: Ashgate, 2000), pp. 20–21.

policy and to work out lines of action where domestic and external considerations could reinforce each other rather than conflict. Moreover, they carried an authority which other ministers did not have'. This was referred to as the 'Rambouillet effect', where multilateral negotiation could be pushed ahead periodically by decisions taken at the highest political level.[5]

1977–2001: The G8 as a Non-Proliferation Actor

The G7 summit of 1977 in London was the first where the group addressed non-proliferation as a security issue. In doing so, the G7 partners committed themselves – in the context of the 'increasing reliance' that 'will have to be placed on nuclear energy to satisfy growing energy requirements' – to 'reducing the risks of nuclear proliferation' and to launching 'an urgent study to determine how best to fulfil these purposes'.[6] Similar statements on nuclear non-proliferation were made in the final *communiqués* of the next four summits from 1978 through to 1981, against the backdrop of the expected expansion in the use of nuclear power and growing concerns about proliferation. Notably, the G7 also pronounced a commitment to providing a reliable supply of nuclear fuel to other countries, particularly in the developing world.[7] In the aftermath of the oil crisis there was a general perception that the nuclear power sector would expand exponentially in size as a means of providing states with greater energy security against oil price fluctuations. The expansion of nuclear power that had begun in the 1960s did indeed continue throughout the 1970s and into the mid-1980s. During this time, the percentage of global electricity production provided by nuclear increased from 1 per cent in 1960 to

---

[5] *Ibid.*, p. 21.

[6] 'Declaration: Downing Street Summit Conference', *op. cit.*

[7] The G8 summits in Bonn (1978), in Tokyo (1979), in Venice (1980) and in Montebello (the Ottawa Summit, 1981) all made reference to promoting nuclear non-proliferation. See 'Declaration: Bonn Summit', Bonn, 17 July 1978; 'Declaration, Tokyo Summit', Tokyo, 29 June 1979; 'Declaration: Venice Summit', Venice, 23 June 1980; 'Declaration, Ottawa Summit', 21 July 1981.

16 per cent by 1986, although this latter figure then remained 'essentially constant' for the following twenty-one years,[8] which was largely due to safety fears following the Three Mile Island and Chernobyl nuclear power accidents in 1979 and 1986 respectively. The issue of reducing the prospects of nuclear proliferation at the same time as providing credible assurances of nuclear fuel supply, and the issue of guaranteeing safe nuclear power generation, are all currently back on the international agenda – especially in the wake of the Japanese earthquake, tsunami and nuclear crisis of 2011 – in the context of the pending nuclear renaissance and the announcements by dozens of states in recent years of new or renewed nuclear power programmes to meet energy security and climate change demands.[9]

A significant influence on non-proliferation efforts in the latter part of the 1970s was the 'peaceful nuclear explosion' (PNE) by India in 1974. This event sparked major concerns over how to control the spread of sensitive dual-use nuclear technology and knowledge to non-nuclear weapon states both party to and outside of the then newly established Nuclear Non-Proliferation Treaty (NPT), which India did not sign up to. Indeed, India had acquired a CANDU heavy-water research reactor from Canada in the mid-1950s and had subsequently used it to produce plutonium for its PNE. It was during the four year period following the Indian test, of course, that the Nuclear Suppliers Group (NSG) was established and which by 1978 included all G7 countries, the Soviet Union and a handful of other European countries on both sides of the Iron Curtain.[10]

---

[8] See *Science Daily*, 'Nuclear Power Worldwide: Status and Outlook', 24 October 2007, <http://www.sciencedaily.com/releases/2007/10/071023103052.htm>, accessed 17 June 2011.

[9] A key part of the current debate is how to constrain the spread of sensitive uranium enrichment and plutonium reprocessing capabilities. See, for example, Yury Yudin, *Multilateralization of the Nuclear Fuel Cycle: The Need to Build Trust* (New York and Geneva: UNIDIR, 2010), p. 81, <http://www.unidir.org/pdf/ouvrages/pdf-1-92-9045-009-G-en.pdf>, accessed 22 July 2011.

[10] 'History of the NSG', Nuclear Suppliers Group, <http://www.nuclearsuppliersgroup.org/Leng/01-history.htm>, accessed 16 June 2011.

While the G7 discussed the implications of the Chernobyl disaster in 1986 and this was addressed in the Tokyo Summit's *communiqué*,[11] no real discussion of non-proliferation issues appears to have occurred again at a G7 summit until 1990. However, during the intervening period the Reagan administration did initiate secret talks with other members of the G7 to establish a multilateral but informal mechanism – outside of the G7 framework but involving all the G7 states – to control the spread of nuclear-capable missiles and associated technology and knowledge. Discussions amongst these countries from late 1982 resulted ultimately in the Missile Technology Control Regime (MTCR), which was officially and publicly announced by each of the seven member states in April 1987.[12]

The easing of superpower tensions with the end of the Cold War, and the subsequent growth in concern over the security challenges posed by CBRN proliferation in Iraq, North Korea and elsewhere during the 1990s, resulted in heightened international unease over the security of CBRN materials and weapons across the FSU – notably in Russia – and the risk these would get into the hands of proliferating states like Iraq, Libya, Iran and North Korea.[13] The substantial inventories of CBRN materials and weapons, much of which were poorly secured and stored in

---

?[11] 'Statement on the Implications of the Chernobyl Nuclear Accident', Tokyo Summit, Tokyo, Japan, 5 May 1986, <http://www.mofa.go.jp/policy/economy/summit/2000/past_summit/12/e12_d.html>, accessed 17 June 2011.

[12] America's G7 partners had been chosen for this endeavour because they were both allies and suppliers of missile technology. The need for such a regime was based on growing levels of missile proliferation in the developing world – including the spread of satellite launch technology and other civilian applications of rocketry – which was perceived to be potentially destabilising in regions such as the Middle East, East Asia and South Asia, and therefore posing a potential threat to American and allied security interests. See Wyn Q Bowen, *The Politics of Ballistic Missile Non-Proliferation* (Basingstoke: Palgrave, 2000), pp. 36–37.

[13] During the 1990s, particularly after the sarin attack in Tokyo in 1995, concerns also began to increase over the potential acquisition of CBRN capabilities from the FSU by terrorist groups.

unsafe conditions, presented an unprecedented set of security, non-proliferation, safety and environmental challenges.

Every G7/G8 summit *communiqué* from 1990 to 2001 made reference to the need to strengthen non-proliferation measures, such as the IAEA safeguards system and the NPT, with the focus very much on preventing the proliferation of CBRN to state actors.[14] Moreover, several summits during the 1990s specifically addressed the non-proliferation, safety and security legacy problems in the former Communist bloc countries.

At the Munich Summit in July 1992, for example, an agreement was reached to offer 'states of the former Soviet Union and of central and eastern Europe' financial support to eliminate the dangers associated with Soviet-design nuclear power plants 'within the framework of a multilateral programme of action'.[15] Some five years later, in 1997, the Chernobyl Shelter Fund was established by the G7, EU and Ukraine.[16] The preceding year, in April 1996, the G7 states and Russia had already held a Nuclear Safety and Security Summit in Moscow. Among other things the G7 states and Russia agreed to a 'Programme on Preventing and Combating Illicit Trafficking in Nuclear Material' to enhance co-operation 'in all aspects of prevention, detection, exchange of information, investigation and prosecution in cases of illicit nuclear trafficking'.[17]

?[14] The *communiqués* from the following summits all made reference to strengthening non-proliferation measures: Houston (10 July 1990), London (16 July 1991), Munich (7 July 1992), Tokyo (8 July 1993), Naples (9 July 1994), Halifax (16 June 1995), Lyon (29 June 1996), Denver (22 June 1997), Birmingham (17 May 1998), Cologne (18 June 1999), Okinawa (21 July 2000) and Genoa (20 July 2001).

[15] 'Economic Declaration: Working together for growth and a safer world', G8 summit, Munich, Germany, 8 July 1992, <http://www.g8.utoronto.ca/summit/1992munich/communique/index.html>, accessed 17 June 2011.

[16] See, for example, 'Chernobyl Shelter Fund, EBRD Factsheet', European Bank for Reconstruction and Development, p. 2, <http://www.ebrd.com/downloads/research/factsheets/csfe.pdf>, accessed 17 June 2011.

[17] 'Moscow Nuclear Safety and Security Summit Declaration', Nuclear Safety and Security Summit, Moscow, Russia, 19–20 April 1996, p. 5.

Another key challenge was the proposed conversion of some 34 tonnes of Russian weapons-grade plutonium into fuel for civilian nuclear reactors, a programme with an estimated cost of at least $2 billion. At the G8 summit in 2000, some $800 million was pledged by Canada, France, Japan, the UK and the US to support the initiative. This project alone was an illustration that, by the turn of the millennium, there remained much to be done to address the CBRN legacy. But this was the only area, prior to 2001, in which substantial non-US effort was collectively harnessed to address a specific CBRN threat.

As the above paragraphs illustrate, the G7/G8 summit process had actively addressed non-proliferation, nuclear safety and nuclear security issues long before Kananaskis in 2002. Over this period, the G7/G8 had steadily emerged 'as an effective centre of global governance'[18] and this, in combination with the changing security environment of the post-Cold War era, helps to explain the group's expanding agenda in these fields during the 1990s and 2000s. However, it was the 9/11 terrorist attacks that created the truly unique circumstances in which it became possible for the G8 states to make a high-level political commitment to allocate an unprecedented amount of resources to reducing the risks and threats posed by legacy CBRN materials, initially in Russia and later in other former Soviet republics, under a new partnership.

US and European Threat Reduction, 1990–2001

Before turning to the post-9/11 period, it is important to briefly review US and European activities related to threat reduction during the 1990–2001 period.[19] Prior to 2002, only the US and the

---

[18] John J Kirton, 'Explaining G8 Effectiveness', in Michael R Hodges, John J Kirton and Joseph P Daniels (eds), *The G8's Role in the New Millenium* (Aldershot: Ashgate, 1999), p. 53.

[19] US CTR efforts have been covered in detail elsewhere and will not be addressed in any level of detail here. See, for example, John M Shield and William C Potter (eds), *Dismantling the Cold War: US and NIS Perspectives on Nunn-Lugar Threat Reduction Program* (Cambridge, MA: MIT Press, 1997).

EU had provided threat reduction assistance of any real scale to Eastern European and FSU countries. Some support was provided by Norway, Japan and Canada, for example, but these efforts, including much of the EU programmes, were directed towards human and environmental aspects of Russian CBRN demilitarisation, and particularly focused on enhancing nuclear safety at both civilian and military facilities. While the 1990–2001 period saw the EU programmes (both European Commission- and EU member state-led) focus on a substantial portfolio of work to enhance nuclear safety, this work has continued alongside new programmes embracing all CBRN challenges. For example, Europe is still supporting major projects related to Chernobyl, and many projects associated with the dismantling of Russian nuclear submarines have a strong nuclear safety element associated with spent nuclear fuel.

The United States has been at the forefront of international efforts to address the security of CBRN weapons and material for over twenty years. Since the early 1990s, Washington has supported a CTR programme which was originally designed to assist FSU countries in dismantling their weapons of mass destruction, securing the associated materials, converting former weapons facilities to non-military uses and redirecting former weapons scientists and engineers.[20] To aid the implementation of arms control agreements such as the Strategic Arms Reduction Treaty (START), CTR also contributed to the dismantlement and destruction of a number of nuclear weapons and their associated delivery systems. The CTR programme was initiated by Congress and is often referred to as the Nunn-Lugar threat reduction programme after the two senators, Richard Lugar and Sam Nunn, who steered an amendment to existing legislation to allow for support to be extended to the Soviet Union. The Nunn-Lugar legislation authorising the United States government to provide

---

[20] Paul I Bernstein and Jason D Wood, *The Origins of Nunn-Lugar and Cooperative Threat Reduction,* Case Studies Series, No. 3, Center for the Study of Weapons of Mass Destruction, National Defense University (Washington, DC: National Defense University Press, April 2010), <http://www.ndu.edu/WMDCenter/docUploaded/cswmd-cs3.pdf>, accessed 17 June 2011.

this threat reduction assistance to the FSU republics was based initially and primarily on anxieties over the safety and security of Soviet nuclear weapons and the expertise associated with them, especially after the failed coup in Moscow in August 1991 and the subsequent break-up of the Soviet Union. The programme later expanded from a $400 million per annum programme in 1993 led by the Department of Defense (DoD) to a multi-agency programme (Defense, State and Energy departments) which, by 2002 (and indeed beyond), totalled some $1 billion per year.[21] This programme has been just a part of the US effort to address CBRN threats, with the State and Energy departments' budgets supporting a comprehensive range of non-proliferation and nuclear security programmes prior to the creation of the GP.[22]

While a few European countries and the European Union supported some limited, ad hoc threat reduction work in FSU countries during the 1990s alongside their nuclear safety programmes, by far the largest effort was undertaken by the US CTR programmes. Despite the significant levels of funding committed by the United States during the 1990s, the sheer scale of the Cold War legacy in the FSU highlighted to both the Clinton and George W Bush administrations, as well as to Congress, the importance of involving the wider international community in providing additional funding and technical expertise to more effectively, and more equitably, address the various threat reduction challenges in the region.

Long before the GP was launched, the EU and a number of European countries had been actively involved in providing assistance to FSU states. In the early 1990s, for example, the UK provided specialised vehicles and containers for transporting nuclear weapons from Belarus, Kazakhstan and Ukraine to Russia at a cost of around £37 million, and in 1998 accepted nuclear material from Georgia to reduce the risk of it going

---

?[21] See Amy F Woolf, *Nonproliferation and Threat Reduction Assistance: US Programs in the Former Soviet Union*, CRS Report to Congress, Congressional Research Service, 4 February 2010, <http://www.fas.org/sgp/crs/nuke/RL31957.pdf>, accessed 17 June 2011.

[22] *Ibid.*

astray.[23] Several European countries and the EU also contributed to the Chernobyl Shelter Fund to construct a new $2.21 billion sarcophagus over the damaged reactor in order to prevent further releases of radioactive particles into the environment. However, the most comprehensive example of European support for threat reduction activities was, and remains, the substantial work backed by the EU through the provision of financial and technical assistance to Russia and other FSU countries since the early 1990s, primarily under the TACIS (Technical Aid to the Commonwealth of Independent States) programme.[24] The majority of the work under the TACIS programme was devoted to nuclear safety projects to limit the risk of accidents in the operation of nuclear installations. This programme also covered activities related to non-proliferation, including projects in the fields of nuclear materials accountancy, illicit trafficking and scientist redirection.[25]

---

[23] 'The G8 Global Partnership: Progress report on the UK's programme to address nuclear, chemical and biological legacies in the Former Soviet Union', First Annual Report, Department of Trade and Industry, November 2003, <http://www.decc.gov.uk/en/content/cms/what_we_do/uk_supply/energy_mix/nuclear/nonprolif/global_threat/reports/ann_repts/ann_repts.aspx>, accessed 17 June 2011.

[24] The 'Technical Aid to the Commonwealth of Independent States' (TACIS) programme was created in 1991 to help member states of the Commonwealth of Independent States (CIS) and Mongolia as they transitioned to become democratic market economies. Work formerly covered by TACIS is now covered under the Instrument for Stability and the Instrument for Nuclear Safety Co-operation.

[25] After the collapse of the Soviet Union several thousands of military scientists with knowledge relevant to the development of CBRN capabilities and their means of delivery were left without employment and income. To mitigate against the risk of having these scientists offer their know-how to terrorists and proliferating states, the EU was instrumental in establishing the International Science and Technology Center (ISTC) in Moscow and the Science and Technology Center Ukraine (STCU) in 1992 and 1993, respectively. The key aim of these centres was to provide opportunities for these scientists to redirect their talents to peaceful activities. Funding was provided via the TACIS programme and later

The largest international co-operation effort prior to 2002 was the support given to the science centres in Moscow[26] and Kiev[27] to provide Russian and Commonwealth of Independent States (CIS) former weapons scientists – particularly those with knowledge and skills related to CBRN weapons and their delivery systems – opportunities to redirect their talents to peaceful activities. These centres were established in 1992 and 1993, respectively, with support from the EU, the US, Japan, Canada and Norway for the Moscow-based International Science and Technology Center (ISTC) and from the EU, the US, Canada and Sweden for the Science and Technology Center Ukraine (STCU). Support for the science centres continues to the present day because they are perceived by a number of GP countries to provide one of the primary means to establish collaborative threat reduction projects across the FSU, especially outside Russia. By 2000, these centres had funded over 1,000 projects involving some 40,000 scientists. By 2010, the numbers of former scientists had grown to nearly 90,000 in research institutes spread across the FSU. Government and private sector contributions to the centres over this period have now totalled some $1 billion.

The Post-9/11 Security Paradigm

While the US, the EU and many of its member states were actively involved in threat reduction work prior to 2001, things seemed to change dramatically following 9/11. It is often said that it is difficult to overplay the political, strategic and economic impact that the terrorist attacks had on the United States and the world at large. One of the most significant and long-term impacts was the permanent raising of international concerns over the

---

?through the Instrument for Stability. Canada, Japan, Russia and the US were also involved in establishing the science centres.

?[26] See International Science and Technology Center, Moscow, <http://www.istc.ru>, accessed 17 June 2011.

[27] See Science and Technology Center Ukraine, <http://www.stcu.int/>, accessed 17 June 2011.

potential nexus of terrorism and CBRN proliferation. The level of destruction, particularly in New York, was seen by most policy-makers as an illustration of the depths to which some terrorist organisations, notably those associated with Al-Qa'ida, were prepared to go in pursuit of their radical, transformative agendas. If such organisations were prepared to kill thousands and to destroy swathes of city blocks using commercial aircraft, then the jump to chemical and radiological weapons, and potentially even to biological and nuclear weapons, was seen by many to be a matter of 'when' and not 'if'.

Senator Richard Lugar summarised well the evolution in thinking during a Senate hearing on the GP in October 2002: 'Eleven years ago, when the Nunn-Lugar program was conceived, the terrorist threat was real, but vague. Now we live in an era where catastrophic terrorism, using weapons of mass destruction, is our foremost security concern'.[28] During the same hearing, John Bolton, Under Secretary of State for Arms Control and International Security Affairs, similarly noted that 'the need and the importance of addressing these problems was certainly highlighted by the events of September 11, and the risk of what terrorist organisations would do if they were able to get their hands on weapons of mass destruction, whether through acquisition of the requisite technology or whether through getting the weapons and delivery systems themselves'.[29]

---

[28] Statement by Senator Richard Lugar, 'A Progress Report on 10+10 Over 10', Hearing before the Committee on Foreign Relations, United States Senate, 107th Congress, Second Session, 9 October 2002, S Hrg 107–799 (Washington, DC: US Government Printing Office, 2003), p. 2. The '10+10 over 10' description was the original label given for the GP: $10 billion of funding from US programmes plus $10 billion from G8 countries and others willing to support the initiative over a period of ten years.

[29] Oral testimony of John Bolton, Under Secretary of State for Arms Control and International Security Affairs, 'A Progress Report on 10+10 Over 10', Hearing before the Committee on Foreign Relations, United States Senate, 107th Congress, Second Session, 9 October 2002, S Hrg 107–799 (Washington, DC: US Government Printing Office, 2003), pp. 9–10.

While the willingness of some terrorist groups and individuals to launch mass casualty attacks was clearly evident, and had been long before 9/11, the capability part of the threat equation was less clear. Of course, American anxiety, and international concern in general, over the possibility of mass effect terrorist attacks harnessing CBRN materials had been on a steady rise since the mid-1990s, following the use of sarin nerve agent on the Tokyo subway by the radical Buddhist sect Aum Shinrikyo in 1995. This attack killed thirteen people and injured around 6,300.[30] Nevertheless, while this attack demonstrated to Japan, the United States and the world at large the potential impact that terrorists could have in using CBRN capabilities, it took the direct attacks against the United States on 9/11, which killed nearly 3,000 people, to generate the necessary political resolve in Washington, working with its partners in the G8, to take bolder action by announcing the GP to address potential sources of CBRN weapons and materials.

It was not long after 9/11 that policy officials from the United States and elsewhere began emphasising that the CBRN legacy in Russia and other former Soviet republics presented a continuing opportunity for non-state actors to harness such a capability. This formed the backdrop for the negotiation and formation of the GP by the G8 states in 2002. Bolton noted in October 2002, for example, that 'building on thoughts that many had, President Bush took the lead in working with G8 colleagues to come up with the 10+10 over 10 program [which was renamed the Global Partnership Programme by the time of the 2002 G8 summit] in effect to achieve close to a doubling of the international resources available for work in the former Soviet Union on these kinds of programs'.[31] In addition to the political direction and impetus provided by the Bush administration, the Canadian government invested a

---

[30] See Japan's National Statement at the Washington Nuclear Security Summit, 12 April 2010, Ministry of Foreign Affairs Of Japan, <http://www.mofa.go.jp/policy/un/disarmament/arms/nuclear_security/2010/national_statement.html>, accessed 17 June 2011.

[31] Bolton, *op. cit.*, pp. 9–10.

significant amount of effort to prepare the ground for the launch of the GP in its role as host of the G8 summit in 2002. Shortly after the launch of the GP in 2002 Bolton recognised Canada's input noting that, 'we owe a particular debt to Canada' because 'without their work, I think we would not have come as far as we did'[32] in terms of setting the initiative up in the first place.

Further, the Nunn-Lugar programme continued to evolve and grow in terms of its geographic scope after 9/11, and by 2010 it continued to receive over $1 billion of congressional funding. As noted by Amy Woolf, over the years the CTR has:[33]

> evolved from an emergency response effort to impending chaos in the Soviet Union, to a more comprehensive threat reduction and non-proliferation effort, to a broader programme seeking to keep nuclear, chemical, and biological weapons from leaking out of the former Soviet Union and into the hands of rogue nations or terrorist groups, to a global programme to address the threat of weapons of mass destruction.

The Global Partnership

The statement that publicly announced the launch of the GP began by framing the challenge posed by CBRN terrorism:[34]

> The attacks of September 11 demonstrated that terrorists are prepared to use any means to cause terror and inflict appalling casualties on innocent people. We commit ourselves to prevent terrorists, or those that harbour them, from acquiring or developing nuclear, chemical, radiological and biological weapons; missiles; and related materials, equipment and technology. We call on all countries to join us in adopting the set of non-proliferation principles we have announced today.

The G8 countries agreed to support specific co-operative threat reduction projects to address non-proliferation, disarmament,

---

?[32] *Ibid.*, pp. 9–10.

[33] Woolf, *op. cit.*

[34] The entire GP text from the Kananaskis Summit is included in Annex A, 'The G8 Global Partnership Against the Spread of Weapons and Materials of Mass Destruction', Statement by G8 Leaders, Kananaskis, Canada, 27 June 2002.

counter-terrorism and nuclear safety issues. The initial geographical focus of such projects was agreed to be Russia where the emphasis would be placed, again initially, on 'the destruction of chemical weapons, the dismantlement of decommissioned nuclear submarines, the disposition of fissile materials and the employment of former weapons scientists'. The focus on these areas related to concerns that terrorist groups could gain access to the huge inventories of chemical and nuclear weapons and associated materials stored in relatively insecure conditions across Russia as well as accessing the expertise of former weapons scientists and engineers. While a number of countries in the FSU and elsewhere also had nuclear facilities requiring assistance to enhance their security, Russia's inventory of Cold War materials presented by far the largest threat, and one which Russia was deemed in 2002 not to be capable of dealing with in a timescale acceptable to the international community. To support projects in these fields the G8 countries agreed to 'raise up to $20 billion' over ten years.[35] Specifically, the Bush administration agreed to spend $10 billion over ten years on implementing the GP and its G8 partners agreed to match that commitment.[36] For a G8 summit this was an unprecedented political commitment of resources to address a series of primarily non-proliferation related challenges. This outcome was largely dependent on the combination of two factors. First, the events of 9/11 had focused the minds of policy-makers on the potential for mass effect terrorism potentially harnessing CBRN materials. Second, eight heads of state pledging their countries to such a major investment of resources demonstrated the importance of the Rambouillet effect.

The Kananaskis agreement was specifically designed to be a flexible framework based on voluntary contributions from supporting countries and it did not establish a new bureaucratic structure with its own staff and infrastructure. In a structural sense, the GP is best described as a G8-endorsed political framework with no overarching legal structure other than a set

---

[35] *Ibid.*

[36] Lugar, *op. cit.*, p. 5.

of six principles and guidelines designed to shape international collaboration on threat reduction.[37] The principles were designed to 'prevent terrorists, or those that harbour them, from gaining access to weapons or materials of mass destruction'. All states were called upon to commit themselves to:[38]

1. Promote the adoption, universalisation, full implementation and, where necessary, strengthening of multilateral treaties and other international instruments whose aim is to prevent the proliferation or illicit acquisition of such items; strengthen the institutions designed to implement these instruments.
2. Develop and maintain appropriate effective measures to account for and secure such items in production, use, storage and domestic and international transport; provide assistance to states lacking sufficient resources to account for and secure these items.
3. Develop and maintain appropriate effective physical protection measures applied to facilities which house such items, including defence in depth; provide assistance to states lacking sufficient resources to protect their facilities.
4. Develop and maintain effective border controls, law enforcement efforts and international cooperation to detect, deter and interdict in cases of illicit trafficking in such items, for example through installation of detection systems, training of customs and law enforcement personnel and cooperation in tracking these items; provide assistance to states lacking sufficient expertise or resources to strengthen their capacity to detect, deter and interdict in cases of illicit trafficking in these items.
5. Develop, review and maintain effective national export and transshipment controls over items on multilateral export control lists, as well as items that are not identified on such lists but which may nevertheless contribute to the development, production or use of nuclear, chemical and biological weapons and missiles, with particular consideration of end-user, catch-all and brokering aspects; provide assistance to states lacking the legal and regulatory infrastructure, implementation experience and/or resources to develop their export and transshipment control systems in this regard.

---

[37] See Chapter III, 'Funding, Prioritisation, Results and Evaluation.'
[38] Kananaskis Summit, op. cit.

6. Adopt and strengthen efforts to manage and dispose of stocks of fissile materials designated as no longer required for defence purposes, eliminate all chemical weapons, and minimize holdings of dangerous biological pathogens and toxins, based on the recognition that the threat of terrorist acquisition is reduced as the overall quantity of such items is reduced.

A number of key issues related to how projects would be undertaken – including project management, legal, contractual and liability issues – were also laid out and resolved collectively between donors and the FSU countries where the projects were to be implemented. These principles were subsequently used by the donors to negotiate appropriate legal agreements with recipients of GP-related financial and technical assistance, and to construct project management frameworks.

A clear goal of the Bush administration in negotiating the GP was to secure much greater funding contributions from its G8 partners – notably in Europe – to support threat reduction work in Russia and elsewhere. At the Kananaskis Summit in 2002 the European Commission subsequently committed to spending €1 billion over ten years on behalf of the EU, including work under TACIS and various initiatives related to non-proliferation under a range of Council Actions.[39] (Since 2006, the main focus of EU work on CBRN risk mitigation has been through the Instrument for Stability; see Annex D).

In terms of burden-sharing, Congress had been applying pressure to have American allies foot a much larger part of the bill. Talking about the GP in October 2002, for example, Senator Joe Biden, then Chairman of the Senate Committee on Foreign

---

[39] The Council of the European Union has provided funding via Joint Actions for a number of CBRN risk mitigation projects and programmes including support to the IAEA Nuclear Security Fund worth some €23 million. Through the Joint Actions, support has been given in the areas of legislative and regulatory assistance, strengthening the security and control of nuclear and other radioactive materials and strengthening national capabilities for detecting and responding to illicit trafficking. This support has been targeted at countries in Central Asia and the Caucasus, Southeast Europe and the Balkan region, Mediterranean countries, the Middle East and Southeast Asia.

Relations, noted that, 'At the very least, it may leverage increased funding on those important projects by our allies in Europe, Japan, and Canada'.[40] Biden even posed a question to this effect, asking, 'Should we increase the current levels of US assistance, or do we envision the Global Partnership only as a means to leverage greater contributions by our allies in Europe, Canada, and Japan?'[41]

Indeed, while the United States may well have continued to support projects in Russia without the GP, the substantial expertise and additional funding secured from other countries under the initiative certainly increased the momentum of international threat reduction work and reassured Washington that other states, notably in Europe, were now more effectively and more equitably sharing the threat reduction burden; the Soviet CBRN legacy was on Europe's doorstep after all and clearly as much of a potential problem for European states as it was for the United States. To leverage further resources and expertise from a wider group of potential contributing states beyond the core G8, it was also agreed at Kananaskis to 'invite other countries that are prepared to adopt its common principles and guidelines to enter into discussions with us on participating in and contributing to this initiative'.[42] Moreover, the G8 specifically committed themselves to broadening the future scope of the GP beyond Russia and the former Soviet Union as a whole. The statement noted that, 'In addition, the G8 would be willing to enter into negotiations with any other recipient countries, including those of the Former Soviet Union, prepared to adopt the guidelines, for inclusion in the Partnership'.[43]

The Kananaskis agreement was key to enabling both G8 and non-G8 countries to secure funding for their GP contributions to CBRN threat reduction over the long term, and

---

[40] Opening statement by Senator Joe Biden, Chairman, Senate Foreign Relations Committee, 'A Progress Report on 10 + 10 Over 10', Hearing before the Committee on Foreign Relations, United States Senate, 107th Congress, Second Session, 9 October 2002, S Hrg 107–799 (Washington, DC: US Government Printing Office, 2003), p. 1.

[41] *Ibid*, p. 2.

[42] Kananaskis statement, 27 June 2002. See Annex A.

[43] *Ibid*.

importantly, to make their own considerable technical and project management expertise available to FSU countries. For example, while the UK was already planning to widen its very limited and essentially ad hoc threat reduction work before 9/11, the attacks were instrumental in persuading the UK, amongst a host of other nations, of the importance of securing CBRN material in a faster timescale than previously envisaged, supported in great part by US funding and expertise. The GP strengthened the case for the expanded UK programme and ensured it had long-term, ring-fenced funding to tackle projects in partnership with other countries, which needed support over several years to be successful. The UK example helps to demonstrate that had the GP not been developed, it is difficult to perceive how the breadth of expertise and funding required to address Russia's Cold War CBRN legacy in a co-ordinated way could have been effectively harnessed.

Conclusion

The GP was not the first non-proliferation initiative to occupy the minds of G8 heads of state. There is a long history of the G8, and the G7 before that, addressing non-proliferation issues, dating back to 1977. Nevertheless, the GP initiative as launched in 2002 was qualitatively different to what had gone before because it involved a substantial commitment of resources over a decade – up to $20 billion and the technical and project management skills of all the G8 countries – to address a pressing set of CBRN proliferation challenges. In this respect, the combination of a new security paradigm post 9/11, typified by the prospect of mass casualty terrorism, with the high-level commitment provided by eight heads of state to address the CBRN legacy problem in Russia and elsewhere proved to be decisive in the establishment of this new initiative. However, Senator Biden struck a timely and prophetic note of caution with regard to the GP in October 2002 when he stated that, 'We cannot allow this important international commitment to dissolve into empty words and failed implementation'.[44] With this warning in mind,

---

?[44] Biden, *op. cit.*, p. 2.

the next chapter examines the extent to which the G8 states have delivered on the priorities identified, and funding pledges made, at Kananaskis.

III. FUNDING, PRIORITISATION, RESULTS AND EVALUATION

While the GP has realised some notable achievements since 2002 – such as providing stability of focus and funding for threat reduction work, destroying thousands of chemical weapons and dismantling over one hundred nuclear submarines, the initiative has failed to adequately address more pressing proliferation challenges. Moreover, not all of the original spending commitments have been met, and the Working Group which was established to 'run' the GP has not proven to be an effective mechanism for prioritising, guiding and evaluating implementation efforts. This failure on the part of the Working Group has been largely due to the consensus nature of its political decision-making process as well as Russia's intransigence *vis-à-vis* permitting the GP to focus on issues and geographical areas not prioritised in Moscow. At this macro-level, then, the past nine years have proven to be something of a mixed bag for the GP.

Funding

Since 2002, a number of G8 summits have been used to launch at least one new initiative related to non-proliferation and the security of CBRN materials. Key examples include the initiative on the security of radioactive materials announced at the summit chaired by France in 2003, the launch of the Global Initiative to Combat Nuclear Terrorism (GICNT) at the Russian-chaired summit in 2006, and an initiative on scientist engagement at the Italian summit in 2009. All have been designed to enhance the momentum of international efforts to mitigate CBRN risks. However, none have included financial pledges to support the initiatives, nor have they sought to foster the sharing of technical and project management expertise between countries to assist one another in improving the security and safety of their CBRN materials. These other initiatives have essentially highlighted the political importance for the G8 countries to collaborate with each other but have not established a financial mechanism to facilitate collaboration. Not only do these other initiatives not have long-term budgets attached to them but, in many cases, they rely on the GP, or other security programme budgets in various countries, for financial support and assistance in the form of related ad hoc projects such as workshops, the provision of technical information, access to specialists and so on. In contrast, long-term financial pledges to fund threat reduction work were at the very heart of the GP as it was conceived in 2002.

High-Level Funding Commitments
A key advantage of having a high-level political pledge by the G8 heads of state which embraced a ten-year timescale was the strong position it arguably provided relevant ministries across the GP countries in seeking to justify and secure budgetary approval from legislators for their threat reduction programmes. All of the GP-related officials consulted in researching this paper believed this was a crucial factor in gaining support for complex and long-term projects. Indeed, several government officials from a number of GP countries have expressed a view that without the GP they would probably not have been able to contribute to global threat reduction and related work outside of their own borders.[1]

Table 1 provides details of the G8 pledges and the estimated levels of spend and contracted commitments up to the beginning of 2010.[2] Importantly, it highlights a mixed record with regard to individual G8 countries meeting their pledges under the initiative. The totals should be seen as approximate because financial data for 2010, as well as previous years, has

---

[1] For example: interview L, written contribution, 1 October 2009; interview M2, 28 May 2009.
[2] As reported at the 2010 G8 summit in Canada.

been poorly collated and not produced in a standardised format, or normalised to one currency or financial year.

Meeting Pledges: A Mixed Record
From Table 1 it is clear that while its spending has fallen in real terms (adjusting for inflation), the US has, in cash terms, maintained a sizeable budget to support threat reduction activities in the FSU and more widely as work in Russia and other former Soviet republics is completed. However, France and Italy stand out because they are on course to fall well below on their funding

Table 1: Pledges made by G8 countries at the Kananaskis Summit for the period 2002–12.

Country	Pledge	Estimated spend and commitments up to 2010*	Estimated percentage of pledge met by early 2010
US	$10 billion	$10 billion	100%
Canada	CA$1 billion	CA$650 million	65%
European Union	€1 billion	€700 million**	~70%
France	€750 million	€135 million	18%
Germany	Up to €1.5 billion	€925 million	62%
Italy	€1 billion	€140 million	14%
Japan	$200 million	$105 million	52%
UK	Up to $750 million	$500 million***	~65%
Russia	$2 billion****	$5.6 billion	280%
Total all states	**~US$20 billion**	**~$18 billion**	

*Calculated from financial data published by the Global Partnership Working Group, 'GPWG Annual Report 2010: Consolidated Report Data - ANNEX A', June 2010, <http://www.canadainternational.gc.ca/g8/assets/pdfs/FINAL%20-%20GPWG%20Report%202010%20-%20Annex%20A%20-%20June%2017%20_2_.pdf>, accessed 14 June 2011.

**Only data on individual programme budgets are presented in the GP annual report – totalling some €550 million. However, these budget figures include some expenditure incurred pre-2002 and also exclude significant contributions to the European Bank for Reconstruction and Development (EBRD) for Chernobyl and work in northwest Russia. The spend figure was provided by the European Commission via a private conversation with one of the authors.

***Although the UK pledge was in US$, its GP returns are in £. The exchange rate conversion for the purposes of this table is £1 = $1.60.

****Increased from $2 billion to $6 billion in 2006 at the 2006 St Petersburg G8 summit chaired by the Russian Federation.

commitments, spending only 15–20 per cent of what they originally pledged. Other major donors – Canada, the EU, Germany, Japan and the UK – have also fallen short of their pledged contributions to date, by between 35 and 50 per cent. The reasons for this failure to deliver are complex and appear to include several factors.

First, establishing projects in Russia turned out to be a very bureaucratic and time consuming process, with some GP countries making little progress in implementing projects for the first three years after 2002. Second, as the Russian economy revived and Moscow's financial position greatly improved some four years after the launch of the GP, a view emerged that Russia itself could now afford to fund such work and did not require G8 assistance at the same levels as agreed at Kananaskis. Moscow's decision in 2006 to increase its pledge from $2 billion to $6 billion – in large part to ensure its chemical weapons facilities would be constructed as close to schedule as possible – reflected the lack of willingness of the GP community to support much more work in this area because of Moscow's improved financial position, as well as the fact that many thought the GP remained too focused on Russia.[3] The decision to increase Russia's own spending commitment also reflected a desire on the part of the Putin government to be seen as less reliant on hand-outs from the other countries in addressing its CBRN challenges. Third, a significant proportion of the French and Japanese pledges were reserved for plutonium disposition work in Russia for which Moscow is no longer seeking financial assistance.[4] When work on Russian plutonium disposition failed

---

[3] GP donor support for chemical weapon destruction projects in Russia is still significant although not as great as Russia had originally hoped for. Some $1 billion has been contributed to the construction of the Shchuch'ye chemical weapons destruction facility by the US, the UK, Canada (together with ten other GP countries), Germany has contributed some €343 million towards the construction of the facilities at Gorny, Kambarka, Leonidowka and Pochep, Canada is committed to contributing some CA$100 million to the Kizner plant and the EU has contributed some €9 million to the Gorny plant.

[4] Interview D1, 6 July 2009.

to materialise, internal budgetary constraints in France and Japan appear to have prevented the two countries from reallocating the funds to other GP projects.

At the end of the Nuclear Security Summit in April 2010, the Obama administration stated that some $18 billion had been allocated by GP partner countries by 2010, including $10 billion from US coffers.[5] Without the extra $4 billion pledge from Russia, the overall $20 billion target would not be met at current expenditure rates. By 2010, the European spend – with the exception of the EU, Germany and the UK[6] – is such that overall pledges are unlikely to be met unless there is a marked increase in project spend in the last year of the current GP period. It could be argued that focusing purely on the financial data can generate a misleading impression of the real impact of donor support for projects on the ground. For example, both France and Italy have made available significant technical expertise to help Russia address its nuclear legacy. Nevertheless, the failure of several G8 countries to deliver on their funding pledges, or to reallocate funds to other tasks when this became necessary, has been a key weakness of the GP. This gives rise to the question of whether the initiative could have been better designed to guarantee that all pledges would be fully delivered.

Given that the Kananaskis agreement was designed to provide a flexible framework, with a limited bureaucracy and voluntary contributions from supporting countries, establishing an EU/UN-type assessed contribution system would have been very difficult, if not impossible, to negotiate: first, because of the urgency associated with setting up the initiative in the first place and, second, because such an approach would have limited the number of GP countries willing to participate as they would have to have agreed to specific sums in advance. In this respect, then, the failure of some donors to live up to funding

---

[5] See National Statement of the United States, Nuclear Security Summit, via US State Department, <http://fpc.state.gov/documents/organization/140353.pdf>, accessed 17 June 2011.

[6] The UK and German G8 GP pledge was prefaced by the words 'up to', but at current rates of expenditure along with the EU programmes are still likely to get close to the maximum figure for the three years 2010–12.

commitments made under international initiatives such as the GP may well be unavoidable and is probably to be expected.

Burden Sharing

Despite the mixed record of turning pledges into actual spending on projects and programmes, the GP has, in the words of one senior European Commission official, 'provided stability of focus and stability of funding' for threat reduction work.[7] This stability has had some positive effects. Perhaps most notably, the burden-sharing nature of the GP was influential in persuading Congress to continue to provide approval for significant American work on threat reduction. The Elimination of Weapons-Grade Plutonium Program (EWGPP)[8] provides a good illustration of where wider GP funding support had a decisive impact on congressional approval for funding. According to senior officials in the National Nuclear Security Administration (NNSA), GP contributions to the EWGPP were instrumental in persuading Congress to allocate the required remaining US finances for this programme to halt the production of over one metric tonne per annum of weapons-grade plutonium in Russia.[9] While it is unlikely that Congress would have ceased all funding for the EWGPP without non-US support, the fact that other GP countries – Canada, Finland, the Netherlands, New Zealand, South Korea and the UK – were prepared to help ensure the Zheleznogorsk reactor was closed before it became an even greater safety concern certainly strengthened the willingness of American legislators to support this work. Department of Energy funding before the provision of international funds averaged around $60 million per year. By 2006 this had increased to $187 million and eventually peaked at $231 million in 2007, nearly four times the funding provided in 2002.

The long-term nature of GP funding has also had a positive impact on the willingness of many non-G8 donors to contribute

---

[7] Interview B4, 15 April 2009.

[8] See the case study on EWGPP in Annex C.

[9] Personal communication with one of the authors (Alan Heyes) when he was Programme Director of the UK Global Threat Reduction Programme.

funding at different stages of projects and programmes, as and when they have been able to because of surplus funds in their own programmes or when convenient opportunities have arisen because it has been possible to gain maximum political benefit both at home and internationally.[10] Such ad hoc contributions from states without their own specific GP programmes to another country's extant programme, via 'piggybacking' arrangements (see Chapter IV), have made up a sizeable element of total GP funding. Recent examples of such ad hoc arrangements include financial contributions from New Zealand, Australia and South Korea for work including submarine dismantlement and the physical protection of nuclear and radiological materials.[11]

Planning Ahead
From the perspective of beneficiary countries such as Russia, Ukraine and Kazakhstan, the long-term nature of GP funding has allowed them to plan ahead with a degree of certainty about the finances they will need to secure themselves, as well as the services and personnel required to complete their specific contributions to projects. Even when a GP donor, or a set of donors, have provided 100 per cent funding for a project this has not meant a 'free ride' for beneficiary countries because they still need to ensure projects meet relevant national standards and comply with domestic regulations. Beneficiary countries have also often needed to allocate resources to monitoring projects and resolving disputes between state agencies that have a stake in a specific activity being undertaken. An example of this requirement can be found in the complex task of making safe

---

[10] Examples here include the Nuclear Security Summit, where a number of GP countries announced funding support for a wide range of projects ranging from securing highly enriched uranium to physical protection of nuclear material and so on. See 'Highlights of the National Commitments made at the Nuclear Security Summit', White House, 13 April 2010, <http://www.whitehouse.gov/the-press-office/highlights-national-commitments-made-nss>, accessed 17 June 2011.

[11] Department of Energy and Climate Change, 'Global Threat Reduction Programme, Seventh Annual Report 2009', 28 March 2010, pp. 50–51.

and secure the spent nuclear fuel from dismantled submarines at Andreeva Bay.[12] There are a number of Russian agencies with an interest in the site, including: the former owners; the Russian Navy (which still operates submarines close to the site); the Russian nuclear regulator, the Federal Environmental, Industrial and Nuclear Supervision Service (Rostechnadzor); the regional government administration; and a number of Rosatom institutes that provide technical advice. Rosatom (Russia's State Atomic Energy Corporation)[13] manages and co-ordinates work at Andreeva Bay through its Federal Center for Nuclear and Radiation Safety. Some of the costs of this monitoring work are provided for by GP donors.[14]

The main economic beneficiaries of GP spending can be divided up into two distinct groups. The first group comprises the private and public sector contractors managing projects in beneficiary countries on behalf of GP donors. These contractors provide the essential project management services to donors and, in most cases, have been selected by competitive tender processes. Exceptions include states such as France and Italy which have used existing public sector agencies to implement GP projects. Similarly, some projects require the purchase and provision of equipment and again, in most cases, these are subject to competitive tenders usually undertaken by the project management teams of GP donor countries. For the European Union, and member states of the EU, the project management work and provision of equipment and services for GP projects

---

[12] See the case study on Andreeva Bay in Annex C.

[13] The State Atomic Energy Corporation 'Rosatom' (SC Rosatom) includes over 250 enterprises and scientific institutions, including all civil nuclear companies in Russia, facilities in the country's nuclear weapons complex, research organisations and the only nuclear-propelled fleet.

[14] GP work in Ukraine and Kazakhstan is also subject to oversight by national regulators. See Foreign and Commonwealth Office, Department of Energy and Climate Change and Ministry of Defence, UK, 'Global Threat Reduction Programme, Seventh Annual Report 2009', pp. 29–30, <http://www.decc.gov.uk/en/content/cms/what_we_do/uk_supply/energy_mix/nuclear/nonprolif/global_threat/reports/reports.aspx>, accessed 17 June 2011.

has to comply with the EU state aid and procurement directives. Similar procurement processes are followed by the Canadian, Japanese and US programmes.

The second group of economic beneficiaries are the contractors and companies in the recipient countries where projects take place. Wherever possible, competitive tendering has been undertaken for construction projects and it is one of the key responsibilities of the donor's project managers to ensure this process meets international standards wherever possible. For some projects, such as submarine dismantlement, no tendering is possible because the submarines are allocated to specific shipyards, usually where they were constructed. For these types of projects, contract prices have been developed through negotiation using the specialist skills of the donor's project managers.

There have been some projects that may best be described as 'tied aid'. Perhaps the most obvious example here is Italy's provision to Russia of a spent nuclear fuel (SNF) transport ship at a cost of some €71.7 million. The vessel is being built in an Italian shipyard to a specification agreed with Rosatom. The fact that Italy is one of the G8 contributors to fall well short of fulfilling its 2002 funding pledge, and has allocated a high proportion of what it has spent to projects in Italy itself, is a little perplexing given the rationale underlying the GP.

For Moscow, the promise of GP funding from other states for its two priorities of chemical weapons destruction[15] and submarine dismantlement[16] served as a strong motivational factor to find its own additional financial and technical resources to commit to threat reduction work.[17] In the process, this has ensured that Russia accepted its responsibility for dealing with CBRN legacy issues within an appropriate timescale that was acceptable to its GP partners. This has been an important political

---

[15] See case study on chemical weapons destruction in Annex C.

[16] See case study on submarine dismantlement in Annex C.

[17] During the Russian presidency of the G8 in 2006, the Russian Federation stated that it was increasing its pledge from $2 billion to $6 billion. The statement was made during a G8 GP Working Group meeting by the head of the Russian delegation. Although no minutes of Working Group

achievement for the GP and it has also demonstrated that Russia has a strong incentive to take seriously its G8 responsibilities. Unsurprisingly, Moscow is currently only focused on addressing its own considerable CBRN legacy priorities, so its broader commitment to G8 values in CBRN risk mitigation will only be fully demonstrated when it begins to contribute funding to projects elsewhere, should the GP pursue a truly global approach to threat reduction beyond 2012. Indeed, there are already signs that Russia is prepared to do this. For example, it is providing significant funding (some $21 million) to the EBRD's Chernobyl Shelter Fund.[18]

Implementation: Limited Horizons

An examination of the extent to which the G8 countries have succeeded in meeting the priorities and objectives identified in 2002 reveals another mixed bag in terms of implementation. Within the priorities identified at Kananaskis it was agreed by the GP that the main focus would be on Moscow's twin priorities of destroying its chemical weapons stocks and dismantling submarines. It was also agreed that the initial focus of projects would be Russia, although the geographical coverage of the recipient base would be expanded in due course with the G8 open to expressions of interest from both potential new recipients and donors.

---

meetings are published, the information was published in the 2007 UK annual GP report. See Foreign and Commonwealth Office, Department of Trade and Industry, Ministry of Defence, UK, 'Global Partnership Fourth Annual Report 2006', p. 7. <http://www.decc.gov.uk/assets/decc/what%20we%20do/uk%20energy%20supply/energy%20mix/nuclear/nonproliferation/global_threat/annual_report/file36547.pdf>, accessed 17 June 2011.

[18] 'Chernobyl Shelter Fund, EBRD Factsheet', European Bank of Reconstruction and Development, <http://www.ebrd.com/downloads/research/factsheets/csfe.pdf>, accessed 17 June 2011. See also the Chernobyl case study.

Russian Priorities

The ability of the GP to focus its collective efforts on addressing the full range of CBRN security and proliferation risks identified in 2002 has been limited by several factors. These include the consensus nature of its political framework, the sheer enormity of the four 'initial priorities', and the fact that Russia – and a number of other GP countries including Norway, Sweden, Finland and Japan – took the view that addressing the environmental impact of the CBRN legacy, particularly with respect to nuclear safety issues, was just as important as dealing with the security and proliferation implications. The result has been, not surprisingly in hindsight, a relatively limited horizon, with the GP's unchanging and primary focus on completing work prioritised by Moscow in the field of chemical weapons destruction, the dismantlement of its decommissioned nuclear submarines, and dealing with the associated spent fuel. The GP was certainly not conceived as an environmental or nuclear safety programme, or one in which much of the resources would be focused on a single country to cut up redundant and rusting submarines, and to destroy chemical stocks which Russia had already agreed to dispose of by ratifying the Chemical Weapons Convention (CWC) some five years before Kananaskis but which it did not have the resources to deliver on without outside assistance.[19]

Bringing Russia into the heart of the G8-GP decision-making process in 2002 did constitute a major political achievement at the time. Moreover, the negotiation and implementation of multilateral initiatives and activities, formal or otherwise, will always require compromises to be reached between the parties involved because of the wide range of national interests that have to be taken into account and reconciled, if only partially, between participating governments. However, as noted by one senior official from a European G8

---

[19] The Russian Federation signed the CWC on 13 January 1993 and ratified it on 5 November 1997.

member state, 'it was not at all clear why all countries allowed Russia to dominate the priorities' in this way.[20] The failure to define the broad intention to implement the programme 'initially in Russia' and Moscow's blocking of the GP adopting a more flexible approach to geographical expansion has had the combined effect of directing some 70 per cent, if not more, of available donor funding to Russian projects.[21] In this respect a senior official from another European G8 member state argued that 'the wording in the Kananaskis documents relating to "initially in Russia" could have been better defined'.[22]

This is a disappointing outcome given that the GP was launched in the wake of 9/11 with the aim of 'preventing terrorists, or those that harbour them, from acquiring or developing nuclear, chemical, radiological and biological weapons; missiles; and related materials, equipment and technology'.[23] The GP evolved as an instrument focused largely on the priorities of a single G8 country, rather than providing a unique opportunity to focus international efforts on issues across the globe of more direct relevance to preventing mass casualty terrorism. Agreeing to Russia's agenda has placed constraints on the funding that could be accorded to more pressing threat reduction priorities. For example, the Russian government de-emphasised the importance it accorded within the GP to plutonium disposition after 2002. Plutonium disposition in Russia had understandably been identified as a top priority in 2002, given the direct applicability of plutonium to the construction of an improvised nuclear device (IND) by terrorists. As noted earlier, this work failed to materialise

---

[20] Interview D2, 6 July 2009.

[21] Calculation based on figures provided within Annex A of the 'Global Partnership Working Group Annual Report, 2010'. It is important to note that the financial labelling system used by the GP Working Group report does not allow for a more accurate calculation of fund distribution.

[22] Interview E1, 2 June 2009.

[23] 'The G8 Global Partnership Against the Spread of Weapons and Materials of Mass Destruction', Statement by G8 Leaders, Kananaskis, Canada, 27 June 2002.

because Moscow stopped seeking financial assistance in this area. Indeed, progress was not really forthcoming on this front until the US and Russia signed a plutonium disposal protocol at the Nuclear Security Summit in April 2010.[24] Other pressing priorities that have been undermined by the focus on those imposed by Russia include: securing nuclear and radiological material outside Russia; scientist redirection and engagement; bio-security and bio-safety; replacing with LEU the HEU fuel that remains in a number of research reactors around the world in order to remove the threat that terrorists could acquire the HEU for the preparation of an improvised nuclear device; providing technical expertise and training to a number of states to enhance their threat reduction policies and embrace more effective export control regimes for dual-use goods; and more effective border monitoring control for detecting the smuggling of nuclear and radiological material.

Destroying Chemical Weapons and Dismantling Submarines

While neglecting these other pressing priorities is a major and valid criticism of the GP, it is nevertheless important to examine the significant progress made possible by the GP in the chemical and submarine fields. Most, if not all, decommissioned submarines have now been dismantled and almost all of Russia's chemical weapons stocks are expected to be destroyed by 2015.[25] This is no mean achievement given the situation in 2002 when over one hundred submarines

---

[24] See 'Signing of the Plutonium Disposal Protocol', 13 April 2010, US Department of State, <http://www.state.gov/secretary/rm/2010/04/140120.htm>, accessed 17 June 2011.

[25] Russia has announced a delay in completing the destruction of all of its chemical weapons from 2012 to 2015 due to technical and funding problems. 'Opening Statement by the Director-General to the Executive Council at its Sixty-First Session', 61st Executive Council Meeting, Organisation for the Prohibition of Chemical Weapons, The Hague, 29 June 2010, <http://www.opcw.org/index.php?eID=dam_frontend_push&docID=13851>, accessed 17 June 2011.

awaited dismantlement and 40,000 tonnes of chemical weapons stocks awaited destruction. Moreover, most of the donor countries had little or no experience of working in Russia and other FSU republics in 2002, and Moscow itself had limited experience of working directly with other countries on often technically complex projects involving hazardous materials, in proximity to and sometimes within sensitive military areas. The main exception, of course, was the US CTR programme, which had been operating successfully across the FSU for a decade by 2002.

Securing G8 support for the expensive task of destroying chemical weapons was a significant achievement for Moscow. Russia was committed under the CWC to complete the process of destroying its chemical weapons stocks by 2012. Although Russia ratified the CWC in 1997, and in doing so committed itself to destroying its chemical weapon stocks, initial progress was slow primarily because Moscow had applied insufficient funding to the task. Destroying its vast chemical arsenal was always going to be a formidable challenge both technically and financially, so harnessing the support of its G8 partners was seen by Russia as a key means through which to meet its CWC commitment. Nevertheless, the emphasis placed by the G8 on chemical weapons was prompted by recognition of the sheer quantity of materials involved, as well as Russia's inability to deal with these challenges in a meaningful timeframe given its limited financial and technical resources at that time. The country's chemical weapons stocks were felt to present a real threat because a high proportion of these stocks were weaponised, with some 30,000 tonnes in the form of nerve agents (sarin, soman and VX) contained in over four million artillery, rocket and air delivered munitions, which were capable of being used in a range of conventional delivery systems. The relative compactness of many of these munitions – some of which would fit into a standard size briefcase, for example – made them a potentially easy target for theft and thus represented both a security and a proliferation risk.[26]

In 2010, Russia announced a delay of up to three years in meeting its CWC commitment and cited budgetary and technical problems as the explanation. Russia's increased funding pledge in 2006 had been influenced by its desire to meet the CWC timetable. It is important to note that the CWC deadline was not based on any precise calculations and the United States is also likely to miss the 2012 deadline for destroying its chemical weapons legacy.[27] Nevertheless, some 20,000 tonnes have already been destroyed in large part because of the momentum created by the GP and the availability of additional funding and technical support from fifteen countries.[28] Most importantly, some 85 per cent of Russia's chemical weapons will have been destroyed by the end of the current ten-year phase of the GP. This is a significant achievement given the complexity and scale of the challenge confronted in 2002. It is also clear that without the financial

---

[26] Russia's chemical weapons destruction facilities are being built close to the seven storage sites to reduce the safety risks of transporting such dangerous materials over long distances. Once the specialised facilities have been constructed, the first step in the construction process is to extract the chemical agent from the munitions by drilling and draining each munition. The drained chemical agent is then treated in a two stage destruction process, the first stage of which is chemical neutralisation of the agent, the 'reaction mass' from the neutralisation process is then incorporated into bitumen, to render it incapable of being converted back into chemical warfare agent. This bituminised material is then contained in drums and permanently stored on site. Metal components from the munitions are then decontaminated, in a special furnace, and subsequently treated as scrap metal.

[27] Michael Nguyen, 'US unable to meet CWC 2012 deadline', *Arms Control Today* (May 2006), <http://www.armscontrol.org/act/2006_05/CWC2012>, accessed 17 June 2011.

[28] Chris Schneidmiller, 'Russia to Miss Chemical Weapons Disposal Deadline', *Global Security Newswire, Nuclear Threat Initiative*, 30 June 2010, <http://gsn.nti.org/gsn/nw_20100630_4072.php>, accessed 17 June 2011.

(~$1.5 billion by 2010), technical and project management contributions made by GP countries, the volume of Russia's chemical weapons stocks still awaiting destruction would be very much larger, and the proliferation threat they posed would have persisted well beyond 2012.[29]

While Russia's decommissioned submarines posed few security or proliferation concerns, the substantial quantities of spent nuclear fuel and other high-level nuclear waste and radiological materials associated with them, either onboard or stored at poorly secured facilities onshore, had given rise to both security and safety concerns. The two key onshore bases where these materials were located were Andreeva Bay[30] and Gremikha in northwest Russia. The Andreeva Bay site, for example, is one of the largest repositories in the world for spent nuclear fuel associated with military activities. The storage tanks for this fuel were in poor condition and no longer weatherproof against rain, snowmelt and ground water penetration before GP projects were implemented. Significant levels of contamination of the ground have been recorded close to these stores and at Gremikha.

Getting the G8 to agree to assist with the dismantling of these submarines was a major achievement for Moscow because Russia did not have the financial and technical resources available to deal with this challenge within a reasonable timeframe. In contrast to the regular maintenance work undertaken on US and UK decommissioned submarines awaiting eventual destruction,[31] many of the Russian submarines had experienced little if any remedial work during the forty years or so of being moored in remote fjords, and

---

[29] For more detail on chemical weapons destruction, see the case study on the UK chemical weapons destruction programme which demonstrates both the benefits of the GP in terms of providing momentum to the Russian chemical weapons destruction programme as well as the positive impact of 'piggybacking'.

[30] See case study on submarine dismantlement in Annex C.

[31] Unlike the UK, the US has dismantled a number of their decommissioned submarines using a methodology similar to that used in Russia – see 'US Nuclear Weapons Cost Study Project', The Brookings Institute, <http://www.brookings.edu/projects/archive/nucweapons/subs.aspx>, last accessed 16 June 2011.

the longer the period without such work, the higher the eventual cost of dismantling them became. A good deal of the spent fuel from the submarines was also damaged and, as argued by some, could potentially lead to an uncontrolled nuclear reaction and subsequent radioactive contamination of the surrounding area, if not properly handled.[32]

The GP work related to submarine dismantlement had a very positive impact, enhancing the project management competence of Russian agencies through their work with GP countries proficient in managing large projects, which should have long-term benefits in terms of enabling Russia to manage future projects more effectively by itself. The projects have also demonstrated to Russian agencies that were formerly suspicious of the motives of some G8 countries that dealing with Soviet nuclear legacies was of great concern to the wider international community, and by working together they could be addressed effectively. This development of confidence and trust between donors and beneficiaries was fundamental to the success of GP projects in Russia.

The dismantling of Russia's decommissioned nuclear submarine fleet is now almost complete, with only three submarines in the far east and one in the northwest of Russia expected to be still awaiting dismantlement by the end of 2011. Two submarines in the far east have been damaged by nuclear accidents and are to be sealed, although not in concrete, and moved to an isolated location where they will remain for several hundred years until radiation levels drop sufficiently to allow safe dismantling, although dismantlement is not actually envisaged. By the end of 2010, 191 submarines had been dismantled, with GP donors contributing funding to around a third of these and Russia itself dismantling the remainder.

The last four submarines are currently being dismantled with GP funding. Canada, the UK and Norway have worked closely together to share technical know-how to enhance safe and effective project delivery. The Canadian submarine dismantling programme has been particularly effective, dealing

---

[32] See for example, Aleksandr Nikitin, 'Andreyeva Bay: Time to Avert a Catastrophe', Bellona Foundation, June 2007, <http://www.bellona.org/position_papers/Andreyeva_bay_catastrophe>, accessed 16 June 2011.

with submarines in both northwest Russia and the Russian far east.[33] In total, European countries (Italy, the UK and Norway) have funded the dismantling of thirteen nuclear submarines.[34] Germany also funded the construction of a major storage facility at Syda Bay, near Murmansk, for the long-term storage of submarine reactor components as well as the cost of preparing a number of reactor compartments for long-term storage. The US has funded the dismantlement of thirty-three[35] submarines (costing $354.7 million up to April 2011) under the 1993 Strategic Offensive Arms Elimination Implementing Agreement with Russia.

Broader Issues and Priorities

Despite the GP's formal rigidity of focus on Russian priorities, a number of donor countries and the EU have supported CBRN risk mitigation projects across the entire FSU and further afield. These have led to improvements in the physical protection of nuclear and radiological materials, helped to retrain former weapons scientists, improved border security capabilities for the detection of illicit trafficking of nuclear and radiological material, made safe and secured tonnes of spent reactor fuel, and replaced highly enriched uranium in a number of research reactors with low-enriched uranium. A number of countries, notably Canada, the UK and the US now count such projects as part of their GP portfolio, even though the recipient countries have not formally signed up to GP principles and guidelines.[36] The UK, for

---

[33] See the case study on submarine dismantlement which highlights Canada's dismantlement programme.

[34] Information provided by the IAEA Contact Expert Group Secretariat.

[35] The last submarine dismantled with support from the US was worked as a 'joint' US, Canadian and Russian effort. Canada defuelled the reactors, the US dismantled the launchers (sixteen SS-N-18 missiles) and Russia dismantled the bow and stern.

[36] For example, the United States Department of State's Export Control and Related Border Security Assistance programme has initiated projects globally, with at least two states on every major continent represented. The UK has initiated nuclear safety projects in Lithuania, Armenia, Bulgaria, Slovakia and Romania, and scientist redirection projects in Georgia and Iraq. Canada has initiated projects in the Kyrgyz Republic. See 'GPWG Annual Report 2009 Consolidated Report Data: Annex A', G8 summit, L'Aquila, Italy, 8–10 July 2009.

example, has supported bio-safety projects in Georgia, Azerbaijan, Armenia and Kyrgyzstan, together with physical protection upgrades for nuclear facilities in Armenia and Tajikistan. The argument for their inclusion is that the projects relate to the principles and goals of the GP and so should be recorded as such in the annual project returns published at each G8 summit.[37] Most of these 'GP-related projects' are being undertaken using legal agreements that, in the main, existed before Kananskis, notably under the IAEA's legal instruments, EC Joint Actions[38] and TACIS (now under the Instrument for Stability), along with various US government bilateral agreements.[39] While some countries have used the GP framework to report other CBRN risk mitigation activities, most have not done so and this has resulted in under-reporting of the true extent of international efforts to address global threats from CBRN materials and know-how.

---

[37] An example of this is the project portfolio presented at the 2010 Canadian summit. See <http://www.canadainternational.gc.ca/g8/assets/pdfs/FINAL%20-%20GPWG%20Report%202010%20-%20Annex%20A%20-%20June%2017%20_2_.pdf>, accessed 17 June 2011.

[38] Although threat reduction projects are undertaken via the EU's Instrument for Stability, a number of EU Joint Actions utilise the IAEA to deliver nuclear security. For example, the EU contribution to the IAEA Nuclear Security Fund via Joint Actions is expected to exceed €30 million by the end of 2010. See 'EU Statement at the Nuclear Security Summit in Washington', 12 April 2010, <http://www.europa-eu-un.org/articles/en/article_9662_en.htm>, accessed 17 June 2011.

[39] For example, the US National Nuclear Security Administration's Global Threat Reduction Initiative (GTRI) programme is undertaking a major portfolio of nuclear security projects ranging from HEU recovery to physical protection upgrades. The GTRI programme has a number of bilateral agreements in place to facilitate these projects and embrace clauses covering site access, taxation and third-party liability. See, for example, National Nuclear Security Administration, US Department of Energy, 'Fact Sheet: GTRI: Reducing Nuclear Threats', 2 January 2009, <http://nnsa.energy.gov/mediaroom/factsheets/reducingthreats>, accessed 17 June 2011.

Scientist Redirection

Immediately after the collapse of the Soviet Union there was concern in both Russia and elsewhere that redundant scientists and other former weapons personnel could potentially sell their expertise to the highest bidder, whether a state or non-state actor. This concern led the US, for example, to support a range of scientist redirection activities under the Nunn-Lugar initiative. A particular concern of many of the G8 states at Kananaskis was the threat that would be posed by former weapons personnel from the closed nuclear cities unless a process of rationalisation and restructuring was implemented to provide redundant personnel with decent civilian employment and new business opportunities for the future.

Addressing the human dimension of non-proliferation, and doing so in a sustainable manner, is a more complex task than addressing the physical security of CBRN materials which, in the final analysis, are the property of specific governmental or non-governmental organisations. The 'ownership' issue when it comes to 'human capital' is obviously a much greyer area and helps to explain the shortfall in attention to redirection under the GP. Unfortunately, and despite the emphasis placed on the human dimension at the Italian 2009 GP summit,[40] only a very limited amount of new work has been initiated on scientist engagement in recent years. A major factor in all of this is the fact that, by the time the GP was implemented, the Russian government no longer perceived its scientists to present a proliferation threat. In large part this was because Moscow took the view that the country was now capable of ensuring the security of its work force and their movements. The Russian government's lack of interest in this field became so entrenched that subsequent international agreements negotiated with Russia after the 2002 summit excluded redirection work for political reasons, despite it being one of the core GP priorities. This had the effect of limiting new initiatives on scientist redirection and

---

[40] GP Working Group, 'Recommendations for a Coordinated Approach in the Field of Global Weapons of Mass Destruction Knowledge Proliferation and Scientist Engagement', G8 summit in L'Aquila, Italy, 2009, <http://www.g8italia2009.it/static/G8_Allegato/Annex_B,2.pdf>

engagement within Russia outside the science centres. Moreover, the Russian government notified the International Science and Technology Center (ISTC)[41] in Moscow that it was withdrawing from the agreement that established the ISTC in 1992.[42] However, with Russia's agreement, the ISTC governing board has recently agreed to continue its work until 2015 to allow the completion of projects and to allow time to shift the main facilities from Moscow to Almaty, Khazakstan.

The Russian government's lack of enthusiasm for scientist redirection was not reflected in the regions directly affected by job losses from former CBRN facilities. Indeed, a number of countries have supported redirection programmes under the GP, including Canada, France, the UK and the US, with others, including the EU, supporting redirection projects at the ISTC in Moscow and the Science and Technology Center Ukraine (STCU) in Kiev.[43] However, only Canada, France, the UK and the US have supported significant work on redirection outside of the science centres. Examples of such work include the US Department of State's WMD Personnel Engagement and Redirection programme in Iraq and Libya; the UK's biological non-proliferation and redirection of WMD expertise projects in Georgia, Iraq and Libya; and the

---

[41] The establishment of the ISTC in 1992 with support from the EU, Canada, Japan and the US was part of the international commitment to provide Russian and CIS former weapons scientists, particularly those with knowledge and skills related to weapons of mass destruction and their delivery systems, opportunities to redirect their talents to peaceful activities. Details of the activities of the ISTC can be found at International Science and Technology Center, <http://www.istc.ru>, accessed 17 June 2011.

[42] See 'Statement of the 52nd Governing Board of the International Science and Technology Centre', 9 December 2010, International Science and Technology Center, <http://www.istc.ru/istc/istc.nsf/va_WebPages/GB52Eng>, accessed 17 June 2011.

[43] The STCU is an inter-governmental organisation set up in 1993 under an agreement signed by Canada, Sweden, Ukraine and the United States; Sweden was later replaced by the EU. The STCU was established to help former CBRN experts in their transition to self-supporting, civilian work in the scientific and business sectors. See Science and Technology Center Ukraine, <http://www.stcu.int/>, accessed 17 June 2011.

French programme to create links between French enterprises and Russian laboratories.[44] Unfortunately, the French programme finished prematurely in 2009[45] due to budgetary pressures on France's GP programme after only eighteen months of operation.[46]

France and the UK have focused specifically on commercialisation with the aim of creating new, long-lasting, non-weapons employment opportunities for former weapons scientists and technicians. The UK programme's target of creating some 3,000 lasting jobs by 2012 is close to being achieved and at least 55 per cent of this figure is made up of former nuclear weapons scientists and technicians in Russia, Armenia, Belarus, Georgia, Kazakhstan, Ukraine and Uzbekistan. The direct provision of European economic regeneration expertise encompassed by these programmes to support remote communities in the FSU would not have been possible without the GP framework. In practice, the EU does not have the means to initiate programmes targeted specifically at closed nuclear cities in Russia and similar nuclear physics institutes in neighbouring CIS countries. It is worth noting that half of the expenditure of the UK programme has been on grants to fund the purchase of equipment and set-up costs (including assistance on finance) for business expansion, which the EU programmes would have found difficult to provide in an integrated fashion with its technical assistance support. EU rules mean that grant funding and the provision of services (such as consultancy, training and capacity building) are never mixed, and this makes it difficult to provide commercial enterprises with grants because of concerns over distorting competition.

---

[44] 'GPWG Annual Report 2009 Consolidated Report Data: Annex A', G8 summit, L'Aquila, Italy, 8–10 July 2009.

[45] The French conversion programme was a commercially focused activity involving European companies and Russian scientists, shaped to become sustainable after four years of operation. Despite the programme's early termination, seventy-five highly qualified jobs should be created and two to three joint ventures implemented. A Russian company, ValoDia, has been created to continue the French conversion work in a private capacity. Information provided by the French conversion programme manager Peter Linholm.

[46] Interview D1, 6 July 2009.

> **Box 3:** Summary of Scientist Redirection Work
> Undertaken via the Science Centres in Moscow and Kiev
>
> Altogether some 73,000 former weapons scientists and other team members in research institutes in Russia and the CIS have been involved in ISTC projects and activities. The total project funding between 1994 and 2009, from all parties, for the ISTC was some $835 million (this includes pre-2002 funding which was therefore not in the GP programme), which was used to support some 2,700 projects and involves approximately 14,000 former weapons scientists and their support teams. More than 400 government organisations and private companies have joined the 'partner programme' to date and have provided funding for 717 research projects, totalling $255 million. The share of funding from European 'partners' amounted to $43 million.[47]
>
> 17,700 scientists and engineers have benefited from funding via the STCU since 1994. Some 10,000 of these were former weapons scientists. As of 18 November 2010, 1,466 projects had been funded, including 866 regular projects, 457 partner projects and 140 projects under Targeted Initiatives. The total amount contributed to STCU projects since 1994 is around $209 million.[48]

Despite the importance accorded by several donors, scientist redirection and engagement has been and will remain probably the most difficult of the GP non-proliferation programmes to evaluate and to determine what the longer-term, sustainable impact of the work will be. While it is clear from the support given to ISTC and STCU that some 90,000 scientists and their team members have benefited from the resources provided via GP-funded programmes (see Box 3), the long-term non-proliferation benefits are less clear. The overriding objective of most, if not all, of the GP programmes in this field has been to limit and then

---

[47] 2009 Annual Report: 15 Years of Science Cooperation, ISTC, p. 59, <http://www.istc.ru/istc/istc.nsf/va_webresources/Annual_Reports/$file/AR%202009%20final.pdf>, accessed 17 June 2011.

[48] Information provided by the Executive Director of the STCU, Andrew Hood, and also taken from the STCU website, <http://www.stcu.int/>, accessed 17 June 2011.

remove the threats and risks associated with the proliferation-sensitive information, knowledge and understanding that was built up across generations of former weapons scientists and engineers. This has been a complex challenge and the commercial viability of redirection projects conducted over a five to ten year timescale may not be the key factor in ensuring non-proliferation objectives are met. Other factors include the exposure of former weapons scientists and related personnel to Western standards of best practice in areas such as project management and adherence to sound environmental and economic practices, and the development of civil society, amongst other things. These other factors may be equally as important in addressing the redirection challenge in the longer term and after GP funding has ceased.

In short, the near-term non-proliferation benefits of ensuring that a few thousand former weapon scientists and engineers had their salaries supplemented for a set period until economic conditions improved in the FSU – by using their scientific and engineering skills in non-weapons related employment – may not be as significant as other factors in strengthening non-proliferation efforts aimed at addressing 'human capital'. Certainly, some assessments of US-funded scientist redirection programmes present mixed views regarding the real and sustainable achievements of such programmes. For example, a 2007 report by the US Government Accountability Office (GAO) on the US Department of Energy's programme related to scientist redirection was critical of its real impact.[49] It noted that 'more than half of the scientists paid by the program

---

[49] See 'Non-Proliferation: DOE's Program to Assist Weapons Scientists in Russia and Other Countries Needs to be Reassessed', US Government Accountability Office, Report to the chairman of the Committee on Homeland Security House of Representatives, December 2007 (GAO-08-189), p. 78, <http://www.gao.gov/new.items/d08189.pdf>, accessed 17 June 2011. Positive assessments of US scientist redirection programmes include D Y Ball and T P Gerber, 'Russian Scientists and Rogue States', *International Security* (Vol. 29, No.4, Spring 2005), pp. 50–77; M S Cook and A F Woolf, *Preventing Proliferation of Biological Weapons: U.S. Assistance to the Former Soviet States*, CRS Report for Congress, Library of Congress, 10 April 2002.

never claimed to have WMD experience' and '10 nuclear and biological institutes in Russia and Ukraine told us that IPP program funds help them attract, recruit, and retain younger scientists and contribute to the continued operation of their facilities'.[50] The audit also threw doubt on the sustainability of the long-term private sector jobs created under the programme. It is clear that the design of future instruments to deliver effective engagement programmes aimed at enhancing professional responsibility for all those possessing sensitive knowledge and expertise will need to consider these intangible aspects carefully.

Environmental Impact
The Northern Dimension Environmental Partnership (NDEP) is an initiative aimed at co-ordinating efforts to tackle environmental problems in northwest Russia, particularly challenges stemming from radioactive waste. The objective of the NDEP is to promote co-ordination between Russia, GP donor countries and international financial institutions to raise funds for priority projects. While most, if not all, of this work is environmental in nature and has a strong nuclear 'safety' rather than 'security' focus, it addresses a key priority of countries in proximity to Russia which view the Cold War legacy as much in environmental terms than anything else. Norway, for example, welcomed the focus of the GP on northwest Russia because it meant that it was no longer alone in addressing the challenges presented by sites such as Andreeva Bay,[51] or the numerous decaying nuclear submarines and other nuclear waste inventories just a few kilometres from the Norwegian border.[52]

The EBRD manages the NDEP fund, which has been a recipient of significant funding as a result of pledges made under the GP. According to one EBRD official, 'without it there would

---

[50] US GAO, *op. cit.*, pp. 5–6.
[51] See case study on Andreeva Bay.
[52] Interview H1, 27 Feb 2010.

probably not have been sufficient money for the Northern Dimension Environmental Partnership's (NDEP) nuclear related work in north-west Russia'.[53] Nine GP countries and the European Union[54] have contributed funding to the EBRD for NDEP work in Russia and more than half of these donors do not have their own threat reduction programmes (see Table 2). The implementation of the GP has therefore enabled a significant amount of funding – some €165.6 million[55] – to be focused on a key environmental and nuclear safety challenge in the fragile Arctic region. This work includes the decommissioning of the heavily contaminated *Lepse* spent nuclear fuel transport ship (€43 m), defuelling of the *Papa* class submarine (€6.5 m), decommissioning a spent nuclear fuel transportation system at Andreeva Bay (€20 m), preparation of a strategic master plan for the clean-up of the nuclear inventory in northwest Russia (€7 m), urgent clean-up projects at the former Russian naval base of Gremikha (€7 m) and radiation monitoring and emergency response systems for the Murmansk and Arkhangelsk regions (€10.2 m). Future projects in the pipeline include further activity to assist in the removal of spent nuclear fuel from Andreeva Bay and the construction of a storage facility for casks containing spent fuel from Alfa class submarines. While the €165.6 million donated so far is insufficient by itself to address all of the necessary nuclear clean-up work in northwest Russia, it is providing invaluable core funding and expertise alongside other GP donor aid and enabling Russia itself to make a good start in developing its own funded programmes.[56]

Had Russia been left alone to deal with such nuclear legacy problems it is very likely that some of the work would not have

---

[53] Interview C2, 28 July 2009.

[54] The EU funding for its CBRN risk mitigation programmes under the Instrument for Stability, and nuclear safety work under the Instrument for Nuclear Safety Cooperation, form the large part of its GP pledge, alongside CBRN risk mitigation work funded under Council Joint Actions.

[55] Made up of €150 million from donors to the NDEP plus €16.6 million gained in interest by EBRD's management of the NDEP fund.

[56] France, Italy, Norway, Sweden and the UK have supported bilateral projects in northwest Russia outside of the NDEP as part of their GP threat reduction programmes.

Table 2: NDEP Support Fund pledges for nuclear projects in Russia.

European Union	€40 million
France	€40 million
Canada	€20 million
Germany	€10 million
Finland	€2 million
United Kingdom	€16.2 million
Norway	€10 million
Denmark	€1 million
Netherlands	€10 million
Belgium	€0.5 million
Total	**€149.7 million***

*Some €95 million have been allocated to Grant Implementation Agreements and contracts with a total value of €28.7 million have been signed. €21.3 million of this had been disbursed by 30 September 2010.

Note: Sweden has pledged €19 million to the general NDEP fund.

Source: European Bank for Reconstruction and Development.

been completed within a reasonable timeframe, or to internationally accepted safety and security standards. For example, due to budgetary constraints and different assessments of risk to those applied elsewhere, Russia may have opted for higher-risk options to deal with spent nuclear fuel and the nuclear waste stored in unsatisfactory conditions in northwest Russia. With some nuclear sites posing environmental as well as potential security risks to other countries in Europe, any nuclear accident or incident arising from cutting corners would potentially undermine public acceptance of nuclear energy strategies currently being pursued in Europe and elsewhere. In this respect the work of the GP has helped to reduce the risks of nuclear incidents, thereby bolstering the prospects for the 'nuclear renaissance', with many governments now placing nuclear energy at the centre of their energy and climate security strategies, despite the 2011 nuclear crisis in Japan.

The availability of GP funding to support activities over a ten-year timescale has also clearly helped governments to mobilise continued support for the ongoing G8-led Chernobyl programmes.[57] The Chernobyl Shelter project alone is estimated

---

[57] See case study on Chernobyl in Annex C.

to cost over $2 billion. These programmes[58] led by the EBRD are vital to completing the decommissioning of the Chernobyl site and the construction of a new shelter to transform the existing one over the destroyed Unit 4 into a stable and environmentally safe condition. The budgets established by donors for GP work are therefore contributing directly to continued progress in making the Chernobyl site safe.

Bio-Security and Radiological Materials
It is evident that the GP has missed the mark on bio-security. Since the release of anthrax-contaminated letters into the US postal system shortly after 9/11, growing international attention has been given to the potential misuse of the biological and medical sciences in the development of biological weapons by non-state actors. Despite the significant growth in concern over biological terrorism in the US and elsewhere, the GP has not focused on this issue in a meaningful way. The GP portfolio has included comparatively few biological-related projects and only Canada, the UK and the US have supported work in this area as 'GP-related projects'. In recognition of this gap, the US has now allocated significant funding to bio-security and the US National Strategy for Countering Biological Threats[59] released in 2009 has accorded a significant priority to related threat reduction work in this field. Canada is also programming significant funds to counter biological threats and other GP donors such as the UK and the EU are starting to focus much more attention in this area.[60]

---

[58] Chernobyl Shelter Fund and Nuclear Safety Account. See 'Nuclear Safety Funds', European Bank of Reconstruction and Development. <http://www.ebrd.com/pages/sector/nuclearsafety/safetyfunds.shtml>, accessed 17 June 2011.

[59] 'National Strategy for Countering Biological Threats', National Security Council, White House, November 2009, <http://www.whitehouse.gov/sites/default/files/National_Strategy_for_Countering_BioThreats.pdf>, accessed 17 June 2011.

[60] Details of specific programmes can be seen in the Annual Global Partnership Consolidated Data project reports. For the 2010 report, see

Moreover, the GP has had only a limited focus on the security of radiological materials.[61] Securing the many thousands of disused and abandoned radiological sources located across the FSU and beyond remains a key challenge in the CBRN field, primarily because there exists no global inventory of radiological materials. Millions of radioactive sources have been distributed worldwide over the past fifty years with hundreds of thousands currently in use and storage. According to the IAEA, for example, more than 10,000 radiotherapy units for medical care are in use; about 12,000 industrial sources for radiography are supplied annually; and about 300 irradiator facilities containing radioactive sources for industrial applications are in operation. The European Commission also estimates that some seventy sources are lost from regulatory control every year in the EU.[62] While the US Global Threat Reduction Initiative (GTRI) and the IAEA Nuclear Security Fund are supporting significant work in this area, and a handful of relevant projects[63] have been funded by some other GP donors, much remains to be done.[64] Although the Nuclear Security Summit in April 2010 focused primarily on making fissile material safe and secure within a four-year

---

<http://www.canadainternational.gc.ca/g8/assets/pdfs/FINAL%20-%20GPWG%20Report%202010%20-%20Annex%20A%20-%20June%2017%20_2_.pdf>, accessed 17 June 2011.

[61] See case study on orphan sources in Annex C, Case Study 4.

[62] See, for example, 'Q&A: Safety and Security of Radioactive Sources', International Atomic Energy Agency, <http://www.iaea.org/NewsCenter/Features/RadSources/radsrc_faq.html>, accessed 17 June 2011.

[63] See the full list of GP projects as of 2010 in the 'Global Partnership Working Group – GPWG Annual Report 2010, Consolidated Report Data, Annex A, 2010', op. cit., in note 21.

[64] See case study on securing radiological sources. Relevant projects include: UK co-operation with the Ukrainian Ministry of Emergency Situations to design a highly active spent source disposal facility at the 'Vector 2' complex; German physical protection upgrades at the Ukrainian State Industrial Enterprise (IZOTOP); and a Norwegian project to dispose of and dismantle radioisotope thermoelectric generators from the Barents Sea Area. See 'GPWG Annual Report 2009 Consolidated Report Data: Annex A', G8 summit, L'Aquila, Italy, 8–10 July 2009.

timeframe, many states agreed at the summit that a key goal should also be the securing of radiological material.[65] Indeed, support for addressing this aspect of the agenda was evidenced by the approximately $10 million pledged by Belgium, Norway and the UK at the summit largely for that very purpose. Most of these commitments were made to the IAEA Nuclear Security Fund.[66]

Evaluating the Working Group

Having focused thus far on the issues of funding, prioritisation and broader threat reduction issues and goals, this final section examines the role of the GP Working Group, including its strengths and weaknesses as a co-ordinating mechanism. The G8 summit statement in 2002 noted that:

> [T]he G8 will establish an appropriate mechanism for the annual review of progress under this initiative which may include consultations regarding priorities, identification of project gaps and potential overlap, and assessment of consistency of the cooperation projects with international security obligations and objectives.

While the GP has not developed a standing bureaucracy or fixed leadership for this purpose, reviews of progress on project implementation by each country are overseen by the Working Group comprising senior G8 diplomats under the chairmanship of an official from the country hosting the annually rotating G8 presidency. The group has generally met around four or five times a year – although officials and contractors responsible for managing specific GP projects and programmes have met more regularly to discuss the progress of joint activity and to share experiences. It is at this working level related to implementing

---

[65] The final *communiqué* stated that the participants 'Recognize that measures contributing to nuclear material security have value in relation to the security of radioactive substances and encourage efforts to secure those materials as well'. See 'Communiqué from Washington Nuclear Security Summit', 13 April 2010.

[66] See 'Highlights of the National Commitments made at the Nuclear Security Summit', White House, 13 April 2010.

and delivering projects that the GP has probably been the most effective. This has included the provision of the essential political support and influence to smooth the working-level implementation of projects, which have often taken place close to, or within, sensitive areas of the FSU.

However, the role of the group as a vehicle for monitoring progress, providing strategic guidance and undertaking detailed evaluations to ensure that lessons learned are widely disseminated across the GP community has been largely ineffective. In large measure this has been due to the consensus decision-making process of the group and the absence of a standing secretariat to provide some consistency from one G8 presidency to the next.

Strategy, Policy Co-ordination and Evaluation
It is evident that the Working Group has spent insufficient time since 2002 deliberating longer-term strategic issues and providing adequate guidance to participating governments on the priority tasks. According to one senior official from a G8 country, 'the GP Working Group was not a particularly effective forum for driving forward new policy approaches largely due to the influence of the Russian Federation and the clear desire of all successive chairs of the Group to present a consensus way forward'.[67] Another official noted that, 'because [the Working Group] spent some 60–70 per cent of its time on agreeing the reporting statements for each Presidency, it could only be a light touch political steering wheel and expecting it to undertake detailed strategic work was wishful thinking'.[68] A senior official from a European G8 member state noted that the Working Group 'had not been effective in driving forward and developing policy'.[69] This perception was reiterated by another GP country official who noted that, 'donor co-ordination on GP issues could be more effective' and 'the GP could do so much more to develop policy issues'.[70]

---

[67] Interview D1, 6 July 2009.
[68] Interview E1, 2 June 2009.
[69] Interview K6, 27 May 2009.
[70] Interview M2, 28 May 2009.

The consensus nature of the group has evidently not been an ideal mechanism for reviewing changing priorities and conducting strategic oversight of work already underway. A more top-down approach may have prevented the development of a largely unco-ordinated portfolio of projects, some of which, with hindsight and as noted earlier, were not priorities. Moreover, there appears to have been little real opportunity for non-G8 GP countries to influence priorities, despite the significant sums of money and expertise that some have committed to projects.[71] Further, the IAEA could also have played a stronger and more useful role in GP discussions given its substantial experience in the field of nuclear and radiological security.[72] Representatives of the IAEA Office of Nuclear Security have to date only attended one group meeting per year with other GP countries, and the agendas of these meetings have invariably been confined to essentially a series of presentations rather than a meaningful discussion of policy issues. Indeed, an outside observer would be forgiven for thinking that the GP structure was designed to keep most activities focused on Russian priorities rather than to consider CBRN risk mitigation priorities on a global and impartial basis.

Much more could also have been done by the participating countries to promote the positive examples of projects implemented across the GP community in order to promote their potential replication in other areas of CBRN work. The group has done little to nothing to promote the best features of the GP operating mechanisms that have effectively underpinned much of its work. The overall effect has been to undersell significantly some of the real and long-lasting achievements of collaboration, such as the creation of strong networks of GP officials and technical experts at the working level which have been responsible for implementing work on the ground, and are considered further in Chapter IV. Moreover, very few donors have produced annual reports, or established other means of communication such as websites, to outline and to justify their

---

[71] Interview L, written contribution, 1 October 2009; interview M1, 28 May 2009.

[72] Interview H1, 27 February 2010; interview E1, 2 June 2009.

GP-related activities and to raise its profile amongst prospective new partners. While the national reports produced annually by Canada and the UK, for example, have been useful for explaining to domestic audiences the significance of the work being conducted, progress on projects and future plans, much greater added value would have been created if annual reports had been published outlining all of these issues for the GP as a whole.

To date, the entire effort of the Working Group has gone into producing a few pages of consensus text each year – which is invariably buried in a myriad of other summit documents – together with a spreadsheet of projects which details only part of the substantial efforts undertaken by GP countries and is characterised by a significant under reporting of their combined threat reduction initiatives and activities.[73] The financial data associated with this project and programme information is also very poorly presented, with little attempt made to present it in a transparent and consistent format. Given the vast sums of money committed under the GP by numerous governments since 2002 – at a time of increasing concern about public expenditure and competing demands for international aid – a more comprehensive assessment of what had been achieved from the existing activities, what gaps remain, and the lessons learned by undertaking them would have been invaluable, especially in terms of helping to shape the establishment of new projects and programmes elsewhere and providing confidence to new donors of the value of participating in such an initiative. Furthermore, little attention has been given to the work of the GP to date in academia and by the media, so the gap in knowledge and understanding has not been filled through other means.

While the group has conducted occasional reviews and evaluations in the past, most recently under the German

---

[73] Only comparatively short statements on progress, and associated project listings, can be found in the documentation of each G8 summit since 2002. The project listings themselves are not produced in a standardised way, making it difficult to determine project expenditure over a number of years.

G8 presidency in 2007 and under the French G8 presidency in 2011,[74] these have been very shallow exercises lacking in significant analysis and largely influenced by the need to reach a political consensus among the G8 partners as well as a lowest common denominator approach to policy-making within the group. Indeed, a senior official from a European G8 member state noted that the Working Group was 'not an effective mechanism to undertake a detailed review and evaluation of the various GP programmes'.[75] It is important to note that the consensus nature of the GP, and Moscow's success in persuading its G8 partners to focus on Russian priorities, has made it very difficult to implement an effective evaluation. Nevertheless, the issue of consensus, the fact that the GP policy mechanism has limited, for political reasons, what could realistically be achieved across the full bandwidth of CBRN risk mitigation activities, the failure to establish an effective framework to measure the impact of its programmes and to implement regular assessments to inform future developments, promote lessons learned and so on have been significant failings. The absence of assessment data that such an evaluation exercise would generate has meant that the strengths and weaknesses of the GP's operation have not been sufficiently transparent to influence changes in approach. Indeed, if an evaluation process had been built into the GP at its inception it would have been an invaluable tool to encourage the redirection of some funding to the other priorities identified in 2002.

Geographical Scope
Russia was the only recipient country to sign up to the GP guidelines in 2002 and, as far as the authors are aware, no other country was given the opportunity to propose itself in such a capacity at the time. However, the G8 countries did state a willingness to enter negotiations with any other potential

---

[74] 'Global Partnership Review', G8 summit document, Heiligendamm, Germany, June 2007, <http://www.g-8.de/Webs/G8/EN/G8Summit/SummitDocuments/summit-documents.html>, accessed 17 June 2011.
[75] Interview K6, 27 May 2009.

recipient countries – including elsewhere in the FSU – for inclusion in GP if they are prepared to adopt the guidelines (see Chapter II). However, only Kazakhstan and Ukraine have since formally signed up as recipients.[76]

The Working Group should, and certainly could, have done more to encourage new donors and potential recipients to participate formally in the initiative. A key failing in this respect is that a formal strategy does not appear to have been developed to encourage and lobby other countries to participate in the GP, and the contacts that have been made in this respect have been ad hoc and apparently undertaken largely by the United States. This lack of strategy is surprising given the recognition by the G8 and the Working Group of the importance of strengthening the initiative by widening its geographic scope.[77] This failure to engage, and formally to include, no more than two additional recipients over a nine-year timescale because of the lack of political consensus to do so contributed significantly to the narrow focus of the GP on Russian priorities. According to one official from a European donor country, 'given the limited scope for the GP to progress at the Working Group level, a lot more could have been done on a bilateral basis' to 'actively seek new GP donors'.[78] Indeed, the failure of the GP to more effectively reach out to non-FSU countries has been a significant shortcoming of the initiative.

Legal Framework
The GP's reliance on legal agreements negotiated between its members to allow for project implementation has limited the

---

[76] The GP is supporting some major projects in Kazakhstan and Ukraine. In Kazakhstan, for example, the US and UK have provided both funding and technical assistance to decommission the B-350 reactor which used to produce weapons-grade plutonium as well as a portfolio of projects embracing scientist redirection and securing radiological sources. In Ukraine the main support of the GP has focused on work at Chernobyl (see case study). A portfolio of projects embracing scientist redirection and enhancing the security of nuclear facilities is also underway.

[77] See, for example, 'Global Partnership Review', op. cit.

[78] Interview K3, 1 June 2009.

extent to which a number of GP countries have been able to lead projects themselves, although – through 'piggybacking' – this has not greatly hindered the dispersal of a significant amount of funding for projects incorporating chemical weapons destruction and dismantling submarines. All legal agreements required for the implementation of the GP are the responsibility of the donor and recipient countries that are involved in specific programmes and projects. With the initial single-country approach, the development of specific agreements to cover third-party liability, access and taxation have only involved those donors contributing their resources and expertise and Russia as the recipient. In addition to a number of bilateral agreements between Russia and several GP donor countries embracing nuclear and chemical projects, the EU negotiated and signed the Multilateral Nuclear Environmental Programme in the Russian Federation (MNEPR) Treaty in 2003, which allows for EU member states and the EC to implement a narrow range of GP projects in northwest Russia focused on submarine dismantlement and spent nuclear fuel safety and radioactive waste management.[79] This agreement and the bilateral agreements Russia negotiated with GP donors, including the UK-Russia bilateral agreement, did not take account of concerns about the security of Russia's considerable fissile and radiological material inventories or work on scientist redirection, two of the other priorities identified in 2002. It is unsurprising, therefore, that

---

[79] Projects covered by MNEPR include securing and cleaning up spent nuclear fuel storage sites and dismantling old decommissioned nuclear submarines. The MNEPR Framework Agreement was signed by several OECD member countries and the Russian Federation in Stockholm, Sweden, on 21 May 2003. It provides a legal framework designed to promote co-operation in the field of the safety of spent nuclear fuel and radioactive waste management in Russia and deals with critical legal issues such as site access and tax exemption. See, for example, 'Multilateral Nuclear Environmental Programme in the Russian Federation', Center for Nonproliferation Studies, Monterey Institute of International Studies, 2003. <http://cns.miis.edu/global_partnership/030604.htm>, accessed 17 June 2011.

Russia has managed to keep the focus of the GP on Moscow's two priorities.

During the Japanese presidency of the G8 in 2008, the UK introduced a draft model agreement to help fast-track future negotiations with potential new GP countries, although it did not appear in the final summit documentation. Again, this illustrates the failure of the Working Group to actively seek out new members and to demonstrate to them the type of legal instruments required to implement new projects. In short, it further highlights the limitations of the current GP structure, notably the requirement of a consensus in order to move the initiative forward.

Conclusion

The GP was launched and developed as a key international policy response to address concerns over the terrorist acquisition of CBRN following 9/11. According to one senior official from a G8 country, 'the GP is an effective mechanism which allows resources of many countries to be focused on key tasks'.[80] Another official from a European government emphasised that 'assisting Russia to solve its problems would not have been done bilaterally and even if it had been undertaken by some it would have received much less money'.[81] The GP has realised some significant achievements, notably in the realm of chemical weapons destruction and submarine dismantlement, but it is a major cause for concern that greater effort has not been given to enhancing the global security of nuclear, radiological and biological material, along with the related knowledge possessed by scientists and technicians at poorly funded institutes across the FSU. The main factor in preventing a more global and targeted initiative was Russia's blocking of any move in this direction. A further problem with the GP has been the failure of some G8 countries to deliver on their initial funding pledges. Moreover, the Working Group has not provided strategic guidance nor has it conducted effective evaluations or initiated

---

[80] Interview I1, 12 November 2009.
[81] Interview E1, 2 June 2009.

serious discussions about evolving issues and priorities. These are all challenges that must be mitigated as the GP moves forward into the future. Before looking ahead, the next chapter highlights several issues at the working level which provide a much more positive account of the GP experience to date.

IV. OPERATIONAL DELIVERY AND SPIN-OFF BENEFITS

It is at the practical project implementation level that the GP has probably been the most effective. Success in this sense has included the creation of a strong network of GP officials and technical experts responsible for their national threat reduction programmes, the development of trust and good working relations between FSU and GP donor countries at the working level, and the acquisition of project management skills by recipient countries. It is also clear that some considerable and unforeseen benefits of the GP initiative have been realised, both in terms of advancing the non-proliferation goals of the G8 community as well as spin-off benefits in other policy areas for some donors.

Threat Reduction Networks

Since 2002, the GP has utilised the considerable array of technical, project and programme management skills that the G8 states and several other countries have brought to the table. While the levels of funding may attract the headlines in the press and policy journals, the access that the GP initiative has provided for FSU countries to specialist advice on a wide range of technical issues is the underplayed but key success story. While some of the projects have been delivered through international bodies such as the IAEA, most have been implemented, managed and delivered by GP countries through their own threat reduction programmes and using their own resources. But these programmes are not working in isolation from one another, with expert networks having developed as a direct result of the GP.

Multi-Partnership Approach

For the first time the GP has established a truly multi-partnership approach to addressing CBRN threats. Examples of GP-related networks include the Contact Expert Group,[1] which has strengthened co-operation between donors working in northwest Russia on GP programme projects. The Shchuch'ye Co-ordination Group has served as a forum for the UK, Russia, Canada and the US to share information about their respective national programmes, with the aim of maximising their synergistic impact in the Shchuch'ye Chemical Weapons Destruction project. The Border Monitoring Working Group was established in 2005 and through it EU, IAEA and US officials have co-ordinated the selection and execution of work at various border crossings, the types of detection equipment, and arrangements for long-term technical sustainability. This co-ordination has resulted in better use of the available resources in selecting equipment suppliers and the delivery of training.

These and other collaborative activities related to the GP have demonstrated a key attribute of the initiative, which is the role it has played in enhancing the co-ordination and collaboration of GP countries in terms of sharing risk assessments, technical knowledge and practices learned in the process of planning and implementing specific projects on the ground. The net effect has been the implementation of a wide array of complex projects and greater confidence that these will be completed efficiently and safely[2] because the most appropriate technical solutions and risk minimisation strategies have been selected.

The establishment of collaborative networks at the working level has helped politicians and senior officials in charge of GP-related budgets to justify projects to national legislatures and the public. A quick summary of official viewpoints on the GP as a practical co-ordination and collaboration mechanism

---

[1] See 'Contact Expert Group', International Atomic Energy Agency. <http://www.iaea.org/OurWork/ST/NE/NEFW/CEG/index.html>, accessed 17 June 2011.

[2] A good deal of the GP project portfolio involves handling often large quantities of hazardous CBRN material with the objective of making it safe and secure before destruction or long-term storage.

demonstrates the perceived utility in this respect. One European official argued that the GP has been influential in streamlining EC funding for CBRN risk mitigation work,[3] while a non-European official emphasised that 'the GP was a testament to how the international community has worked together to address CBRN issues'.[4] A senior official from an EU member state argued that 'the sharing of information with others and the transparency the structure offered was of great value'.[5] An official from one GP country noted that the mere presence of the GP actually 'inspired them to do more work on threat reduction',[6] while another thought it was 'a fantastic mechanism to provide a picture of what others were doing on threat reduction, sharing lessons learned and avoiding duplication of effort'.[7] On this latter point, the GP has evidently established a highly efficient 'network' for sharing best practice in risk assessment related to proposed projects in FSU countries where few governments and contractors had much experience of operating prior to 2002, and certainly little knowledge of international standards of best practice on risk assessment and project management. One European government official noted that 'through the mechanism of the GP they had been able to achieve the specific objectives of their country'.[8] Another European official highlighted that 'the GP had allowed for detailed discussions on what's been done, what to do in future, information sharing and best practice'.[9]

Without the sharing of technical expertise and the willingness of all participants to share often sensitive information and knowledge, some of the technical challenges associated with addressing the nuclear legacy of the Cold War could not have been addressed in an appropriate timescale. One example has involved the technically complex challenge of safely and securely moving some 30 tonnes of highly radioactive spent

---

[3] Interview B4, 15 April 2009.
[4] Interview J2, 15 April 2010.
[5] Interview E1, 2 June 2009.
[6] Interview H1, 27 February 2010.
[7] Interview K3, 1 June 2009.
[8] Interview E1, 2 June 2009.
[9] Interview B2, 15 April 2009.

nuclear fuel at the former Russian Navy base at Andreeva Bay.[10] Working together, contractors and nuclear specialists – from Russia, the UK, Italy, Sweden, Norway and the EBRD – developed a plan for Andreeva Bay which should enable the safe removal of the spent fuel by around 2014 once the necessary infrastructure has been established. Without the GP, it is highly unlikely that the close working relationships and network of contacts that developed amongst the technical experts from these countries – with proficiencies in nuclear engineering, nuclear safety and nuclear decommissioning – and Russian nuclear engineers and scientists would have been possible. All the nuclear facilities in northwest Russia and the Russian far east associated with GP projects are close to active Russian Navy bases and there are tight security controls in place for visiting project sites. Similar controls are in place for visiting Russian nuclear institutes working with GP contractors, with access dependent on projects in place. Without GP projects there is no access and the collaboration and interactions between Russian nuclear experts and GP nuclear experts would not have taken place.

A specific example of sharing best practice involved Canadian access to Royal Navy salvage expertise, which proved invaluable for its substantial submarine dismantlement programme in northwest Russia and in the far east. The use of heavy lift vessels (HLV) to transport submarines over long distances with guidance from Royal Navy salvage experts greatly reduced the environmental and safety risks inherent in moving these fragile vessels to their dismantlement location. In the process it also demonstrated that such freighting activity is both safe and commercially viable. It is difficult to imagine that this would have happened without the political framework that the GP provided to the Royal Navy, given that its expertise was applied in operations in sensitive military areas of the Barents Sea and which also involved Russian Navy personnel.

The partnership approach epitomised by Andreeva Bay was built on a great deal of bilateral and multilateral interaction and involved a process of confidence-building, during which GP

---

[10] See case study on Andreeva Bay in Annex C.

contractors and government officials on all sides came to trust and respect one another. Moreover, the UK example demonstrates that positive working relationships and networks could be developed and sustained despite the political tensions that developed between the UK and Russia following the poisoning of Alexander Litvinenko with the radionuclide polonium-210 in 2006. Indeed, this event resulted in no significant disruption of the UK's GP work in Russia.

Project and Programme Expertise
Through the transfer of project and programme expertise by international project management contractors, the GP also has had a very positive impact on the future ability of FSU countries to manage threat reduction projects and programmes independently. Pertinent examples involve the work of Crown Agents in providing a building for the long-term storage of spent nuclear fuel from icebreakers in Murmansk which currently cannot be reprocessed, as well as work by Nuvia Ltd associated with spent nuclear fuel from submarines at Andreeva Bay[11] in northwest Russia.[12] The transfer of such expertise means that beneficiary countries should be able to ensure that their own self-funded projects in the future will be better managed through the adoption of international standards of best practice. This is a significant legacy for the FSU countries[13] when they begin to use their own taxpayers' money to implement CBRN risk mitigation projects after GP funding comes to an end.

Importantly, the robust project and programme management skills needed to deliver major capital projects, such as chemical

---

[11] See case study on Andreeva Bay.

[12] Details of the work of Crown Agents and Nuvia Ltd for the UK GP programme are described in the successive Global Threat Reduction Programme annual reports of the UK from 2004–09.

[13] Details of projects funded in the FSU by GP countries as well as Russia can be seen in the annual returns of the GP published after each summit. See 'GPWG Annual Report 2010 Consolidated Report Data - ANNEX A', June 2010, <http://www.canadainternational.gc.ca/g8/assets/pdfs/FINAL%20-%20GPWG%20Report%202010%20-%20Annex%20A%20-%20June%2017%20_2_.pdf>, accessed 17 June 2011.

weapons destruction and the dismantlement of nuclear submarines, have simply not been available from international organisations like the Organisation for the Prohibition of Chemical Weapons (OPCW) and the IAEA. Prior to the launch of the GP in 2002, there did not exist a co-ordinated mechanism to widen burden sharing and to bring together the requisite expertise to tackle such complex projects. Indeed, the development of a GP network of threat reduction experts as well as project and programme personnel has arguably been one of the biggest successes of the initiative.

Support to Established Institutions and 'Piggybacking'

Despite pledges of some $10 billion by more than twenty countries, on top of the existing $10 billion-plus US budget, only a small number of the largest donors decided to establish dedicated national threat reduction programmes with the requisite project management, programme management and CBRN expertise to enable them to become 'intelligent customers' for their own programmes. Although all of the G7 countries established their own programmes to deliver most of their nuclear projects, France, Canada and the EU channelled their funding for chemical weapons destruction at the Shchuch'ye facility through the UK-managed programme.[14] Of the GP countries which were not in the G7, Sweden and Norway, while supporting their own programmes, also provided funding for projects managed by others, notably the UK for work on submarine dismantlement at Andreeva Bay.[15] With the exception of Norway and Sweden, most GP governments decided instead to provide all their funding to established international organisations or to support projects managed by other countries (see the 'Piggybacking' section later in this chapter).[16] This aspect highlights the flexibility of the GP framework and its value in terms of encouraging international burden sharing. Two international institutions in particular have benefited from this approach: the IAEA and the EBRD.

---

[14] See case study in Annex C.
[15] See case study.
[16] See expenditure table at Annex F.

The IAEA

Several countries have committed funding under the GP to the IAEA Nuclear Security Fund (NSF).[17] In March 2002, the IAEA Board of Governors approved a three-year plan of activities in the field of nuclear security and the creation of a voluntary funding mechanism, the NSF, to which IAEA member states were called upon to contribute. The NSF was established to support, amongst other things, the implementation of nuclear security activities to prevent, detect and respond to nuclear terrorism.[18]

Implementation of the IAEA's rolling Nuclear Security Plans is almost wholly dependent on the donation to the NSF of extra budgetary funds and in-kind contributions. Although a few GP countries, including the UK, the US and Canada, have directly supported projects to enhance the physical protection of facilities where nuclear and radiological material are stored, a growing feature of the GP's work in this field has involved a number of donors contributing funds to the NSF. At the Nuclear Security Summit in April 2010, for example, Norway, Belgium and the UK used the occasion to announce further contributions to the fund. Some of these contributions have been part of the funding pledged by these countries under the GP, providing further evidence that the GP framework has enabled donors to react quickly in terms of allocating funds to address CBRN challenges, especially when these are linked to high-level political initiatives. For example, the Nuclear Security Summit was held some three months before the Canadian G8 summit and was designed by the Obama administration, at least in part, to add momentum to the process of refocusing GP efforts away from Russia and towards the goal of securing fissile material on a global basis. Moreover, the NSF enables GP contributing states to support projects in countries where they do not have any legal arrangements to do

---

[17] See case study on orphan sources in Annex C.

[18] For a recent analysis of the IAEA's nuclear security role, see Jack Boureston and Andrew K Semmel, *The IAEA and Nuclear Security: Trends and Prospects,* Policy Analysis Brief, Stanley Foundation, December 2010, <http://www.stanleyfoundation.org/publications/pab/Boureston_SemmelPAB1210.pdf>, accessed 17 June 2011.

so by utilising instead the legal framework provided by the IAEA.[19] In summary, then, the contributions to the NSF have allowed GP states to directly address one of the key principles of the Kananaskis agreement: to 'develop and maintain appropriate effective physical protection measures applied to facilities which house such items, including defence in depth; provide assistance to states lacking sufficient resources to protect their facilities'.[20]

The EBRD has been another recipient of significant funding as a result of pledges made under the GP. According to one EBRD official, 'without it there would probably not have been sufficient money for the Northern Dimension Environmental Partnership's (NDEP) nuclear related work in north-west Russia', the fund of which the EBRD manages.[21] Involvement in multilateral programmes of the type managed by the IAEA and the EBRD has also provided many GP states with an opportunity to learn from, and to influence, much bigger projects than they would otherwise have been able to support by themselves.

'Piggybacking'

In addition to channelling funds through the IAEA and the EBRD, the GP's 'piggybacking' mechanism has enabled one or more donors to channel GP-labelled funds through a lead donor to manage projects on their behalf. This mechanism has been highly effective in enabling smaller donors to participate in the GP because it has maximised, on the whole, the proportion of funds spent on project implementation rather than on overheads. The EWGPP[22] led by NNSA, and the Shchuch'ye Chemical Weapons[23]

---

[19] For example, the UK has contributed to NSF security upgrades at the radioactive waste repository near Fayzabad, Takijistan, and security upgrades at the Armenian Nuclear Power Plant. See Department of Energy and Climate Change, 'Global Threat Reduction Programme', <http://www.decc.gov.uk/en/content/cms/what_we_do/uk_supply/energy_mix/nuclear/nonprolif/global_threat/annual_report/annual-report.aspx>, accessed 17 June 2011.

[20] See Annex A for the entire text of the GP launch statement in 2002.

[21] Interview C2, 28 July 2009.

[22] See case study on EWGPP in Annex C.

[23] See case study on chemical weapons destruction.

portfolio of projects led by the UK Ministry of Defence, are two examples of successful piggybacking projects that have involved several donors.

The UK has implemented procurement and construction projects in support of the chemical weapons destruction facility at Shchuch'ye on behalf of Canada and several other donors, most of whom did not possess their own bilateral agreements with Russia. In doing so, piggybacking has enabled more rapid implementation of projects because it has capitalised on extant arrangements so that time and money has been saved by donors not having to negotiate new arrangements.

From a political perspective, piggybacking has also resulted in shorter time lapses between pledges and the disbursement of funds. From a donor perspective, piggybacking has enabled contributions to be made to programmes that would not otherwise have been considered, given the administrative burden placed on donors stemming from the requirement to negotiate bilateral agreements with recipients and to manage project implementation. From a recipient perspective, piggybacking has simplified the process of working with donors by dealing with just one party rather than a number. For the lead donor responsible for managing a project, piggybacking has allowed for the planning and delivery of larger and more complex projects, and for more rapid project delivery than would have been the case if only its own funds had been available.

The upshot has been that the overall effectiveness of the GP assistance programmes in question has been increased. Furthermore, where donors have been able to make use of each other's technical expertise there has been further scope with piggybacking to enhance the management and co-ordination of projects to the mutual benefit of donors and recipients alike. Indeed, the piggybacking approach certainly increased the scale and impact of the chemical weapons destruction programme in Russia.[24]

Yet piggybacking has had some drawbacks, including the potential loss of political visibility for donors and their loss of direct management control. Moreover, in some cases this approach may also have led to higher management costs because

---

[24] Interview K3, 1 June 2009.

of the need to provide information to a number of donors with different reporting requirements and frameworks for selecting contractors.

Nevertheless, without the piggybacking mechanism it is most unlikely that many of the non-G8 GP countries would have been able to contribute funding, given the administrative burdens associated with establishing the requisite legal agreements to operate in Russia and the project management infrastructure itself. Countries such as South Korea, New Zealand, Australia, the Czech Republic, Belgium, the Netherlands and Ireland have all provided useful contributions to GP projects through such arrangements (see Annex F). Examples include: the $10 million contributed by Australia to Japanese-led submarine dismantlement projects in the Far East of Russia; $250,000 donated by South Korea to submarine dismantlement projects led by Canada and Norway; the financial support received by the UK for its Chemical Weapons Destruction portfolio of projects at Shchuch'ye[25] from ten countries and the EU (see Table 3); and the $30 million contributed by six countries[26] to the EWGPP[27] led by NNSA. According to one official, 'piggybacking was a very effective mechanism to enable countries without the manpower or technical expertise, to support and manage GP projects'.[28]

Spin-off Benefits

While the GP has focused specifically on reducing CBRN risks and threats, there have been several spin-off benefits, many of which have been considerable and unforeseen.

Opening Up

One of the main achievements of the various redirection programmes conducted under the GP has been the way in

---

[25] See case study on chemical weapons destruction in Annex C.

[26] Canada, Finland, the Netherlands, New Zealand, South Korea and the United Kingdom.

[27] See case study on EWGPP.

[28] Interview M1, 28 May 2009.

Table 3: UK Chemical Weapons Destruction project spend at Shchuch'ye (£ 000s).

Belgium	£166
Canada	£51,263
Nuclear Threat Initiative (a US NGO)	£581
Czech Republic	£292
EU	£2,677
Finland	£561
France	£4,283
Ireland	£80
Netherlands	£3,488
New Zealand	£696
Norway	£1,867
Sweden	£432
United Kingdom	£24,212
Total project spend under the programme led by the UK Ministry of Defence	**£90,598**

Source: Seventh Annual Report 2009, UK Global Threat Reduction Programme.

which they have contributed to the opening up of the Russian scientific community and the creation of links both within the community and to the broader international scientific community. These programmes have also helped weapons-related personnel adjust to new realities through training and other instruments. The work of the science centres has been particularly notable in contributing to these outcomes[29] and so it

---

[29] See 'Redirection of Former Weapons Scientists', Foreign Affairs and International Trade, Canada, 2009, <http://www.international.gc.ca/gpp-ppm/former_scientists-anciens_scientifiques.aspx?lang=eng>; Waclaw Gudowski, 'ISTC Partner Program: Gateway to collaboration with Russia/CIS. Minimizing the risks of failure', Thematic Conference on Bio-, Nano- and Space Technologies, EU and Science Centers Collaboration, Ljubljana, Slovenia, 10–12 March 2008; European Commission, Director General for Research, 'ISTC and STCU: Cooperation and Innovation in the Life Sciences', 2006, p. 20, <http://ec.europa.eu/research/iscp/pdf/biotech_brochure_en.pdf>, accessed 17 June 2011; Lothar Ibrügger [Rapporteur], 'Report of the Sub-Committee on the Proliferation of Military Technology: Technology and Terrorism', NATO Parliamentary Assembly, 2002, <http://www.nato-pa.int/default.asp?CAT2=0&CAT1=0&CAT0=576&SHORTCUT=256>, accessed 17 June 2011.

is all the more disappointing that Russia has withdrawn its support from the ISTC.

Trust and Heightened Awareness

As with the wider GP programmes, one of the strengths of the scientist redirection work has been the mechanism that it has provided donor states for engaging with stakeholders in the FSU. Speaking at the Council on Foreign Relations in November 2005, then Senator Barack Obama made this very point about the US CTR programme:[30]

> Part of the strength that I saw of the CTR program was it gives a means of us engaging with the Russians in a constructive way and at multiple levels, not just at the top levels, but you know, you have military officers, intelligence officers who are in a cooperative-joint venture several layers down. And that kind of interaction around constructive common projects does a couple of things. One, it gives us, I think, better intelligence, not in a cloak and dagger sort of way, but simply a presence on the ground and relationships with people that are important in the government. And I think that as we build trust on issues where we have mutual agreement, which allows us in a respectful but consistent and dogged way to push some of these broader issues related to democratization and liberalization.

This type of interaction has produced intangible benefits. According to Kenneth Luongo and William E Hoehn, for example, these have included 'an improved Russian appreciation of nonproliferation; heightened levels of trust between US and Russian officials, military officers, and scientists; and new political linkages and relationships not thought possible during the Cold War'.[31]

---

[30] Richard G Lugar and Barack Obama, 'Challenges Ahead For Cooperative Threat Reduction', Council on Foreign Relations, The Washington Club, Washington, DC, 1 November 2005 (rush transcript, Federal News Service), <http://www.cfr.org/publication/9138/>, accessed 17 June 2011.

[31] Kenneth N Luongo and William E Hoehn III, 'Reform and Expansion of Cooperative Threat Reduction', *Arms Control Today* (June 2003), <http://www.armscontrol.org/act/2003_06/luongohoehn_june03>, accessed 17 June 2011.

Wider Benefits of GP Work
It is important to note that the direct benefits of the GP's work in
progressing threat reduction in Russia have, in some instances,
had important spin-off benefits for other GP countries. This is a
significant aspect of the GP because of the large amount of
resources committed by many governments to the initiative and
the need for them to fully justify such commitments to legislators
and their publics.

Some countries have benefited directly from the exchange
of technical expertise with Russia. For example, a number of
British officials and contractors have highlighted the practical
importance to the UK of undertaking GP projects involving the
dismantling of nuclear submarines because it has provided
invaluable knowledge and understanding of how to dismantle
the Royal Navy's own decommissioned nuclear submarines more
efficiently. To date, the UK has not dismantled any of its
decommissioned nuclear submarines that are currently moored
in the Devonport and Rosyth naval dockyards; most of these
submarines have been de-fuelled and are in a safe condition.
The UK Interim Storage of Laid-Up Submarines (ISOLUS)
programme[32] will eventually dismantle twenty-seven nuclear
submarines, seventeen of which will be redundant by 2012, with
another ten due to be decommissioned over the following
decade. The UK approach so far has been to keep its
decommissioned nuclear submarines well maintained afloat
while detailed planning and consultation is undertaken on
the best options for their eventual dismantlement. The four
submarine dismantling projects in Russia which the UK has
financed, one in collaboration with Norway, have provided
a detailed understanding and first-hand experience of the
dismantling process, from the removal of spent fuel to final
long-term storage of the reactor compartments.[33] This
knowledge will prove to be invaluable in the near future as the
process of dismantling Britain's nuclear submarines begins in
earnest, while lessons learned from the UK's participation in the

---

[32] Submarine Dismantling Project, <http://www.submarinedismantling.
co.uk/Background.html>, accessed 17 June 2011.
[33] Interview K3, 1 June 2009.

project are being fed directly into the ISOLUS programme. The leisurely pace of UK plans to dismantle its decommissioned submarines highlights the effectiveness of the maintenance programme to keep them in a safe condition until a cost effective plan for their destruction is finalised. The current financial pressure on budgets in the Ministry of Defence may well push the submarines' eventual destruction date even further into the future. However, while they present little risk to the environment under the current care and maintenance regime, their physical presence close to Plymouth and Rosyth may well raise public concern if the ISOLUS programme is not seen to be making progress in the next few years. The knowledge gained through the joint decommissioning of Russia's nuclear submarines will be invaluable in carrying out the UK's own decommissioning efficiently.

Another example has involved the Royal Navy benefiting directly from participation in the Arctic Military Environmental Co-operation (AMEC) agreement. Using GP funding, this has enabled the Royal Navy and NATO to undertake a project with Russia to survey the sunken Russian nuclear submarine *B-159* in the Barents Sea, and another project on transporting damaged and fuelled nuclear submarines via a commercial HLV. These projects have been conducted in close partnership with the Russian Navy and have maximised all sides' ability to learn from previous catastrophic accidents. The projects have also provided invaluable knowledge with which to enhance future nuclear risk management mechanisms for nuclear submarines operating in a marine environment. A further benefit has been the opportunity created by the project for enhanced defence diplomacy between the two navies, which should have long-term security benefits for both countries. However, the momentum of AMEC collaboration has now been lost due to organisational changes within Russia's Ministry of Defence, with the consequent loss of further potential benefits to the UK of such direct interaction with the Russian Navy.

The wider benefits to the UK of the GP programme are summarised in the text box on the following page; many of these benefits apply equally to a number of other GP countries both in Europe and further afield.

Box 4: Benefits and Achievements of the UK's Global
Partnership Work

- Gradual reduction in the proliferation, security
  and safety threats to the UK from WMD materials and know-
  how
- Enhancements to global security culture as the GP programme
  raises awareness of the importance of best practice in safety,
  security and non-proliferation
- Contributed to a US-led programme which led to the early
  closure of Russian reactors producing 1.5 tonnes of weapons-
  grade plutonium every year
- Helped Russia to ensure some 3,000 former weapons scientists
  have sustainable non-nuclear jobs that will lower the chance
  that they choose to work for states of concern
- Through work supporting submarine dismantling projects in
  Russia, the UK has gained first-hand experience of direct
  relevance to its future plans to dismantle its own fleet of
  decommissioned submarines in the most cost effective and safe
  manner
- Through AMEC, the Royal Navy has strengthened links with the
  Russian Navy and enhanced best practice for dealing with
  nuclear submarine accidents
- The risk of nuclear incidents at Russian nuclear power plants
  has been substantially reduced through the application of
  international best practice
- Strengthened political relations with partner donors (especially
  the US, Canada, Norway and Sweden) and Russia at both
  governmental and working levels. GP co-operation has
  remained untainted by difficulties in UK-Russia relations
- Helped secure $1 billion US funding for Russian chemical
  weapons destruction, provided a mechanism for a dozen other
  donors to contribute to Russian chemical weapons destruction,
  and helped secure Russian commitment to destroying its
  chemical weapons stockpiles.

Most importantly, significant progress has been made in
securing disused radiological sources.[34]

---

[34] See case study on orphan sources in Annex C, Case Study 4.

Conclusion

Part of the GP's success at the working level has been down to the initiative's informal and innovative approach to implementing threat reduction projects, whether through direct support to established institutions such as the NSF of the IAEA, or via the piggybacking mechanism where useful synergies have been realised amongst funding partners with common objectives. The sharing of best practice in risk assessment and project management, among other things, has also been one of the hallmarks of the GP's effectiveness as a mechanism for multilateral co-ordination and collaboration in threat reduction. The next chapter concludes the paper by considering the future of this multilateral threat reduction under the GP.

V. THE FUTURE OF MULTILATERAL THREAT REDUCTION

This paper has argued that the GP has so far focused excessively on projects in Russia which have been of marginal relevance to the most pressing CBRN security and proliferation concerns. Despite the ability of Russia to fund its own programmes, it has vetoed those that have been of the greatest security interests to other countries in the GP, and dragged its feet on expanding the initiative's geographical focus. Moreover, the GP has yet to achieve its ambitious goals for spending, with even maintenance of the previous decade's overall spending level only made possible by increased European funding to top up the US's contribution, which was being reduced in real terms. While a focus on budget size alone clouds some of the real and positive impacts that the GP programme has had on reducing CBRN threats over the past few years, most G8 countries have fallen behind on their pledges. The exception has been Russia, which increased its pledge in 2006 in the face of growing unwillingness on the part of other countries to subsidise a fellow G8 state with a growing energy economy. While a number of states had sound environmental, as well as security, reasons for wanting to see Russia deal with its Cold War legacy on a faster timescale, and provided financial as well as considerable technical support for this, levels of spending may fall further as a result of the global financial crisis. At the same time, the world faces many new global challenges to which the successful multilateral networks and mechanisms pioneered under the GP, and outlined in Chapter IV, could make major contributions.

Indeed, given sufficient commitment, the GP, with its political influence and financial clout, could become the hub of CBRN risk mitigation and further enhance the effectiveness of international efforts to remove the threat posed by CBRN materials and know-how. However, if the GP is to survive and to realise this vision then it will need to undergo a radical overhaul. Since Kananaskis there has been growing international recognition that the threat of CBRN material being procured and misused by non-state actors encompasses a broader set of issues and geographical locations than those addressed during the first nine years of the GP. The emerging paradigm is characterised by more diffuse and geographically widespread CBRN risks typified, for example, by the pending 'nuclear renaissance' where nuclear materials, technology and know-how look set to spread to dozens of new countries in the years ahead, many of which are located in regions like the Middle East and Southeast Asia that have been beset by problems of instability and terrorism.

Now that the GP states have agreed to extend the initiative's mandate beyond 2012 and expand its membership, this final chapter examines how the GP framework could best be adapted and applied to prevent terrorists and proliferating states acquiring CBRN material and know-how. The decision to extend the GP should make it easier for President Obama and his successors to persuade Congress to continue funding a significant proportion of the international effort on CBRN risk mitigation because of the burden-sharing approach of the GP. As noted earlier, the contributions of other GP countries since 2002 have helped to ensure that Congress has continued to allocate significant funding to CBRN projects on a global scale.

Renewing the GP

The G8 and other GP participants had been considering if and how to renew the GP's mandate for several years prior to the Deauville Summit in May 2011. For example, the US, Canadian and British governments had clearly hoped that a renewed commitment to the GP would have been agreed at the Canadian G8 summit in Muskoka in June 2010 to take it forward for an additional decade and address global rather than Russian priorities. Instead of the expected renewal of the GP with a global focus in the summer of 2010, as discussed at the previous summits in Italy (2009)[1] and Japan (2008)[2] – and despite successive summit statements pouring praise on the GP's achievements and President Obama's stated readiness at the Nuclear Security Summit in April 2010 to commit an additional $10 billion over ten years to GP work[3] – the G8 leaders were unable to reach agreement on extending the initiative at the Canadian summit.[4] While the decision not to renew in 2010 was portrayed by a number of observers as a severe setback for CBRN risk mitigation,[5] the Canadian summit statement cited the lack of an evaluation as a reason for the failure to renew.[6] In doing so, the G8 heads of state agreed to 'ask our senior experts to evaluate the results of the GP to date, as a point of departure for

---

[1] 'Report on the G8 Global Partnership', G8 summit, L'Aquila, Italy, 8–10 July 2009, <http://www.g8italia2009.it/static/G8_Allegato/REPORT_ON_THE_G8_GLOBAL_PARTNERSHIP,2.pdf>, accessed 22 July 2011.

[2] 'Report on the G8 Global Partnership', G8 summit, Hokkaido Toyako, Japan, 7–9 July 2008, <http://www.mofa.go.jp/policy/economy/summit/2008/doc/pdf/0708_12_en.pdf>, accessed 17 June 2011.

[3] In a statement on the Nuclear Security Summit the Obama administration stated that 'We are ready to join with our Canadian colleagues and call for another ten-year extension with an expanded scope/mission and to commit up to another $10 billion towards new projects, including expanding our efforts to improving nuclear security to countries not previously eligible for G8 assistance.' See 'Nuclear Security Summit National Statement of the United States', Office of the Press Secretary, The White House, 13 April 2010.

[4] 'G8 Muskoka Declaration: Recovery and New Beginnings', G8 summit declaration, Canada, June 2010, <http://canadainternational.gc.ca/g8/assets/pdfs/2010-declaration_eng.pdf>, accessed 22 July 2011.

[5] Fissile Materials Working Group, 'Setback for WMD security', *Bulletin of the Atomic Scientists*, 3 July 2010, <http://www.thebulletin.org/web-edition/columnists/fissile-materials-working-group/setback-wmd-security>, accessed 17 June 2011; 'G-8 Nonproliferation Program Faces Uncertain Future', *NTI Global Security Newswire*, 16 August 2010, <http://www.globalsecuritynewswire.org/gsn/nw_20100815_3867.php>, accessed 22 July 2011.

[6] 'G8 Muskoka Declaration: Recovery and New Beginnings', *op. cit.*

developing options for programming and financing beyond 2012, focusing on nuclear and radiological security, bio-security, scientist engagement and facilitation of the implementation of UN Security Council Resolution 1540, as well as the potential participation of new countries in the initiative'.[7] If the absence of an evaluation to guide decision-makers did indeed prevent them from extending the GP in 2010, an obvious question arises: why was an evaluation not commissioned before the summit? A detailed mid-term evaluation around 2008–09, if commissioned, could have provided the required information to assist decision-makers in 2010. Despite the claim that the lack of an evaluation explains the non-decision at the Canadian summit, other factors also appear to have contributed to this outcome.

First, it is important to note that some of the G8 governments are currently facing severe financial constraints, given the impact of the global economic downturn on European economies and related government expenditure. This fact – combined with a view that Russia in particular is now strong enough financially to deal with its own CBRN legacy challenges – undoubtedly influenced many at the 2010 summit to delay a decision. Second, most, if not all, GP countries wanted to have a clear strategy in place before they consider committing further funds. Third, the fact that France and Italy are on course to fall well below their pledges was one of the reasons which influenced Germany not to sign up to an extension of the GP in 2010. Fourth, the failure of the G8 formally to sign up to a much wider range of countries with interests and influence outside the FSU (for example, China, India and countries in the Middle East and Southeast Asia) probably did not help the case for extension in 2010 either. With all these factors, and with the stated need for an evaluation, it is perhaps unsurprising that the Canadian government failed to secure the consensus needed to extend the GP for a further ten years at the G8 summit in 2010.

Some twelve months later, however, the G8 did agree to extend the initiative at the French summit in late May 2011; but on the thorny financial issue no new funding commitments were provided at Deauville and it was agreed that the GP partners would

---

[7] *Ibid.*

in future 'identify activities and decide on funding on a national basis'.[8] More generally, the Deauville Declaration stated:[9]

> We welcome the concrete achievements and measurable results of the Global Partnership against the Spread of Weapons and Materials of Mass Destruction launched in Kananaskis in 2002 for a 10-year period. We remain committed to completing priority projects in Russia. Our assessment of the Partnership recognises the significant progress the 23 Partners have achieved on the full range of WMD non-proliferation activities worldwide. The assessment also provides directions for the future. As such, we agree to extend the Partnership beyond 2012, based on the areas of focus enunciated at Muskoka (nuclear and radiological security, bio-security, scientist engagement, and facilitation of the implementation of UNSCR 1540). We will work with all Partners in discussing assistance needs and coordinating possible projects in the above-mentioned areas, and we will expand membership of the Partnership. Partners will decide on funding of such projects on a national, joint, or multilateral basis.

At the summit it was agreed that if the GP is to remain effective in addressing the CBRN threat, it 'must evolve' with an emphasis placed on 'reforming its focus, improving its coordination, and widening its membership'. In particular, it was noted that the GP should become a 'mechanism for the identification and analysis of third countries' assistance needs, upon their request, in their endeavours against WMD proliferation', and it should also serve as 'a group for the assessment of the capabilities and skills its various members are able to contribute, either individually or collectively delivery of this assistance' in co-ordination with mechanisms such as that provided by the 1540 Committee. Moreover, the summit recognised that priorities are likely to change in the future and that the GP partners 'will further assess and share information, as appropriate, on risks and needs in

---

[8] 'G8 Global Partnership: Assessment and Options for Future Programming', G8 summit, Deauville, France, 26–27 May 2011, <http://www.g20-g8.com/g8-g20/g8/english/the-2011-summit/declarations-and-reports/appendices/g8-global-partnership-assessment-and-options-for.1354.html>, accessed 21 June 2011.

[9] 'Deauville G8 Declaration', G8 summit, Deauville, France, 26–27 May 2011, p. 21, <http://www.whitehouse.gov/sites/default/files/uploads/deauville_declaration_final_-_eng_8h.pdf>, accessed 21 June 2011.

more concrete terms in order to maximize the effectiveness in programming for an extended Partnership'. In terms of expanding the geographical scope of the GP, the G8 agreed that it 'should involve a larger number of stakeholders able to contribute to the fight against WMD proliferation and should think of engaging other countries such as China, India, Brazil, and South Africa, to enlarge the GP'.[10]

In light of the decision at Deauville to extend the GP beyond 2012, the remainder of this chapter examines some of the key issues, challenges and priorities that need to be addressed as the initiative moves forward; some of which were highlighted by the G8 in May 2011, and others not.

New Regions, New Players

As noted by the G8 states in May 2011, if the GP is to be successful in the future in addressing CBRN threats on a truly global basis, then its membership needs to be expanded. This will need to include new players in key regions such as North and Southeast Asia, Africa and the Middle East and to work in partnership with them to enhance the regions' CBRN risk mitigation strategies. To date, some twenty-two countries and the EU have been involved in the GP but their contributions and policy preferences have largely focused on addressing Russian priorities, many of which were also clear priorities for some other GP states but often for reasons unrelated to proliferation or concerns about the security of materials. Generally speaking, it is unlikely that many of the countries involved in GP projects will have a strong policy interest in moving it towards a more diversified and global approach unless a direct national interest can be identified for doing so. EU GP countries that do not have their own threat reduction programmes, for example, would have a strong case to argue that the CBRN risk mitigation programmes under the EU Instrument for Stability[11] make a

---

[10] 'G8 Global Partnership: Assessment and Options for Future Programming', *op. cit.*

[11] See Chapter II and Annex D.

sufficient contribution to international threat reduction and so additional support via the GP would be unnecessary. The EU programmes certainly have an increasingly global reach and embrace many of the key GP priorities, including export controls on dual-use goods, illicit nuclear trafficking, scientist redirection, bio-safety and bio-security, and an innovative approach to establishing 'Centres of Excellence' to further promote CBRN risk mitigation best practice.[12] This is perhaps one of the reasons why some of the G8 leaders could not be persuaded to extend the GP until 2011,[13] despite the fact that a number of other non-G8 GP donor countries would have probably welcomed an extension before the recent French summit.[14]

Beyond the existing GP partners, of course, 'going global' will create opportunities to involve other states both within and in proximity to new countries and areas of concern, and from whom new funding and expertise can be tapped. There is certainly consensus amongst the current GP states that any new members should play an active role in contributing funds and technical expertise. It seems eminently sensible to include in the GP all countries capable of advancing its goals and using their influence to establish projects and networks in priority regions and countries of concern.

One of the key lessons learned from working in Russia, Kazakhstan and Ukraine has been the importance of acquiring a robust understanding of the legal and cultural framework of recipient countries, along with a sound knowledge of their priorities, before initiating any projects. This approach will also be essential in reaching out to new partners. The involvement of China because of its strong regional influence in North and Southeast Asia, and increasingly in Africa, will be essential to ensuring the effectiveness of the GP in addressing global CBRN

---

[12] See Commission of the European Communities, 'The Instrument for Stability Multi-Annual Indicative Program 2009–2011', 8 April 2009 C (2009) 2641, p. 55, <http://ec.europa.eu/europeaid/how/finance/documents/eidhr/ifs_ip_2009_2011_en.pdf>, accessed 17 June 2011.

[13] Of the GP countries only the US, UK, Canada and EU's Instrument for Stability programmes have sizeable threat reduction projects outside the FSU.

[14] Interview H1, 27 February 2010.

threats in the future. However, it is inconceivable that China could be involved on the same basis as non-G8 GP partners have been with the present approach. It is clear there have been few opportunities for non-G8 GP countries to influence priorities, despite the significant sums of money and expertise that some have applied to GP projects which in some cases, such as Norway, have been almost equal to the financial and technical contributions of G8 countries.

One approach to this structural weakness would be to separate the GP from the G8 framework to allow China, India and other key countries in South America, the Middle East and Southeast Asia to become involved directly. Such an approach could also increase the influence of some existing GP members that have strong economic and political links with countries in these regions. Australia and South Korea, for example, have strong political ties in Southeast Asia. One advantage of this is that it could link in potential new funding streams and allow for GP projects to be fast-tracked in other regions. In this vein, it has been suggested that the GP could be moved from the G8 to the G20 framework.[15] However, the possible disadvantage of widening the scope to the G20 is that it could potentially constrain the flexibility of the GP and further add to the problems created by the current consensus-based approach. So, any widening of the GP's membership will need to be approached with a parallel examination of how to make decision-making more effective and responsive.

Widening the membership and scope of the GP will require careful management to ensure that the lessons learned from implementing projects in Russia are built upon and that the Working Group is restructured to facilitate a more effective role in steering a global portfolio of activities. Given the limitations of the group, it will be essential beyond 2012 for it to adopt a more strategic approach to prioritising projects and to providing a more effective assessment and reporting structure. It will also be important that all future members contribute both financially and, ideally, technically to demonstrate their commitment to the

---

[15] Interview O, written submission, 26 November 2009; interview J7, 2 December 2009.

GP as the only such multilateral instrument to implement and co-ordinate CBRN risk reduction activities on a global scale.

One option to avoid the constraints that have been evident since 2002 in relation to the Working Group would involve establishing separate but networked regional steering groups and associated technical support frameworks. In this way, GP donors would have the flexibility to channel their available funds to regions and states which they feel are most needy in terms of supporting CBRN risk mitigation. Regional activities could then be reported to the Working Group at appropriate intervals. Within such a framework future key roles of the GP Working Group could include: identifying priorities in each region; encouraging the sharing of lessons learned from implementing activities across each region; promoting achievements and activities; and undertaking periodic impact assessments. The latter would be of particular importance in demonstrating the effectiveness of multilateral threat mitigation programmes and their wider impact.[16] A more proactive approach like this would help the GP to overcome many of the deficiencies in the operation of the Working Group to date, as highlighted in Chapter IV.

Challenges and Priorities Beyond 2012

In addition to involving new regions and players, and making the GP decision-making process more strategic and responsive, there are several challenges and priorities that will need to be tackled, some of which were highlighted at the Deauville Summit.

---

[16] These wider impacts embracing environmental issues, nuclear safety and public health (as well may be the case with threat reduction work focused on bio-safety and bio-security), together with enhancing the sharing of best practice and resources across a range of issues, can significantly increase the value for money aspects of undertaking threat reduction work. Some GP countries such as Germany and Italy also used their GP funding to provide commercial opportunities for their industries to supply equipment for projects in Russia.

Changes in Scale

One of the biggest challenges facing the GP is likely to involve managing the transition away from large-scale projects focused on legacy nuclear and chemical weapons projects in one country, under a single legal framework and with only one language to think about,[17] to a diffuse range of much smaller projects – both in size and funding requirements – in countries scattered across several regions characterised by different cultures, languages, legal frameworks and political traditions. While many of the large-scale projects pursued since 2002 have been ideal for establishing piggybacking relationships, this approach may not be as suitable for smaller projects. Nevertheless, it would appear likely that opportunities for some piggybacking on nuclear security projects run by, and through, the IAEA will continue for the foreseeable future, especially given the complexity of establishing legal agreements between GP donors and target countries.[18]

Nuclear and Radiological

The Nuclear Security Summit in April 2010 concluded by identifying the key nuclear security threats that the international community needs to address over the next four years, notably in relation to securing fissile materials.[19] As reflected in the 2011 summit documentation on the GP, most if not all of the work necessary to address these challenges could be approached under the GP, as

---

[17] Even though a number of GP projects have been outside Russia, most of these have been in FSU countries with similar legal and cultural frameworks which enabled lessons learned from working in Russia to be of some value. This would not necessarily be the case in seeking to translate lessons learned from working in Russia to implementing projects in, for example, Southeast Asia.

[18] It is probably only on projects involving the safety and security of nuclear materials where robust legal agreements are necessary to protect donor countries. A good deal of future activity on threat reduction will be aimed at awareness raising, transferring best practice, training and so on; 'engagement activities' rather than legacy issues.

[19] See 'Communiqué from Washington Nuclear Security Summit', 13 April 2010, <http://www.america.gov/st/texttrans-english/2010/April/20100413171855eaifas0.6155773.html>, accessed 17 June 2011.

could the concerns raised by a number of world leaders at the summit about the disposition and security of radiological materials. Although the summit was primarily focused on fissile material, the final *communiqué* did emphasise the importance of addressing the global inventory of disused radiological materials and the poorly secured radiological sources in use around the world. Indeed, one key outcome of the summit was the financial commitment pledged by a number of states to the IAEA's Nuclear Security Fund to enhance the security of such sources.[20] These types of commitment demonstrate that the renewed GP could make a significant contribution towards securing the fissile and radiological materials identified at the summit in a meaningful timescale by supporting the IAEA and channelling funds through the NSF, rather than approaching the issue on an ad hoc basis at G8 summit meetings. A more balanced funding profile for the NSF would also enable the IAEA to plan its nuclear security assistance programme much more effectively.

Bio-threats

As noted in Chapter III, while the initial main emphasis at the Kananaskis Summit was placed on nuclear and chemical issues in Russia, international concerns have steadily grown since then over proliferation-sensitive, dual-use information associated with the bio-technology industry and with both emerging and re-emerging infectious diseases.[21] While some GP countries, notably the US, the UK and Canada, have initiated projects in these areas, much greater thought and effort is required in the GP context to take forward the bio-security agenda. For example, outreach activities need to be designed and delivered that can

[20] See 'Highlights of the National Commitments made at the Nuclear Security Summit', White House, 13 April 2010, <http://www.whitehouse.gov/the-press-office/highlights-national-commitments-made-nss>, accessed 17 June 2011.

[21] See, for example, *Biotechnology, Weapons and Humanity* (British Medical Association and Harwood Academic Publishers, 1999); 'Public Health Response to Biological and Chemical Weapons' in second edition of *Health Aspects of Chemical and Biological Weapons: Report of a WHO Group of Consultants* (Geneva: World Health Organization, 2004);

enhance risk mitigation in the public health sector on a global basis. The breadth of specialisms required to support a co-ordinated capacity building programme in CBRN public health risk mitigation is such that no single donor is likely to be in a position to provide it all. Consequently, a mechanism needs to be found to attract involvement by a range of potential donors. The GP framework is an ideal one through which to foster and promote such collaboration in close consultation with the groups such as the World Health Organization (WHO), the World Organisation for Animal Health (OIE) and the Food and Agricultural Organization of the United Nations (FAO).[22] A key objective should be to create a public health and agricultural health response framework through which co-ordinated capabilities across the CBRN field can be applied in the event of a bio-incident to establish rapidly the type of agent involved and, based on this, to deploy the requisite containment, medical and

---

Life Science Research: Opportunities and Risks for Public Health: Mapping the Issues (Geneva: World Health Organization, 2005) WHO/CDS/CSR/LYO/2005.20; 'A More Secure World: Our Shared Responsibility', paragraphs 68–70, submitted to the UN Secretary-General on 1 December 2004, Secretary-General Note, A/59/565, 2 December 2004; National Research Council (US), Committee on Advances in Technology and the Prevention of Their Application to Next Generation Biowarfare Threats; *Globalization, Biosecurity, and the Future of the Life Sciences*, (Washington, DC: National Academies Press 2006) – also known as the Relman Report.

[22] WHO 'is the directing and coordinating authority for health within the United Nations system. It is responsible for providing leadership on global health matters, shaping the health research agenda, setting norms and standards, articulating evidence-based policy options, providing technical support to countries and monitoring and assessing health trends'; see 'About WHO', World Health Organization, <http://www.who.int/about/en/>, accessed 16 June 2011. OIE 'is the intergovernmental organisation responsible for improving animal health worldwide'; see 'About us', World Organisation for Animal Health, <http://www.oie.int/eng/en_index.htm>, accessed 16 June 2011. FAO 'leads international efforts to defeat hunger'; see 'About FAO', Food and Agricultural Organization of the United Nations, <http://www.fao.org/about/en/>, accessed 16 June 2011.

environmental countermeasures. More specifically, an important role, again working in conjunction with other international and regional bodies, would be to extend support to capacity building projects in the area of laboratory bio-safety and bio-security, and associated activities such as the transport of potentially infectious material as well as emergency preparedness and response. Similar to the nuclear agenda, a global approach will be required which encompasses key regions such as Africa and Southeast Asia. The scale of the global economic and political impact of serious infectious disease spreading from a single region (for example, SARS, avian 'flu, swine 'flu) demonstrates the need to support the development of early diagnosis and alert capabilities in some regions.

Chemical Industry

Beyond the destruction of legacy chemical weapons stocks, an area of growing concern in the context of CBRN terrorism is the potential vulnerability of the dual-use chemical industry to being targeted by terrorist groups. In 2007, for example, insurgents in Iraq acquired chlorine normally used for water purification purposes and used it to launch attacks in conjunction with conventional explosives.[23] The GP could potentially provide a useful framework through which to raise awareness of the security issues associated with chemical materials used in a wide range of industrial processes. As access to CBRN weapons materials becomes more difficult as a result of the work of the GP and other threat reduction initiatives, terrorist groups interested in non-conventional weapons may opt to seek access to industrial chemicals that are subject to less stringent security arrangements, but which could nevertheless potentially be harnessed for malign purposes. While weaponising chemicals is not a straightforward task, sabotage of chemical plants or transports may represent a simpler task for determined terrorist groups. Preventing terrorists from acquiring such materials is likely to become an increasingly important task in the future, as

---

[23] See Richard Weitz, Ibrahim Al-Marashi and Khalid Hilal, 'Chlorine as a terrorist weapon in Iraq', *WMD Insights*, May 2007.

tighter controls are put in place for nuclear and radiological materials and as bio-safety and bio-security international standards of best practice are increasingly taken up.

Scientist Engagement

The future focus of threat reduction in the field of 'human capital' is likely to shift from addressing former weapons scientists and engineers to engaging scientists and engineers not working in the weapons field but who have dual-use expertise relevant to the manufacture of CBRN weaponry. In agreeing the GP's extension beyond 2012 the G8 did highlight the centrality of ensuring a 'responsible approach toward development and use of sensitive technologies and knowledge' in the context of advances in science and technology and growing exchanges of materials and knowledge on a global basis.[24] Indeed, the emphasis here will need to be on promoting professional responsibility in terms of awareness of, and adherence to, international standards of best practice in the handling and securing of sensitive materials and information. This is likely to be a major task and involve working closely with science and engineering academies, professional institutions and agencies such as the IAEA, OPCW and the WHO. Such an approach will constitute a paradigm shift in how the human dimension of proliferation is approached at the multilateral level, and a future GP could potentially have a central role to play in co-ordinating international work in this area. While the GP does not have a strong track record in terms of evaluating the impact of its work – beyond counting the number of submarines dismantled and tonnes of chemical weapons destroyed – there could be an important role to play in this area in terms of helping to define metrics for assessing the impact of any non-proliferation and other security programmes developed on a global basis to meet this challenge.

---

[24] 'G8 Global Partnership: Assessment and Options for Future Programming', *op. cit.*

Resolution 1540
Finally, at the 2011 summit the G8 highlighted the future role that the GP should play in 'facilitating the implementation of UN Security Council Resolution 1540'. Taking a more proactive role in assisting countries to meet their obligations under UNSCR 1540 – which established binding obligations on states under Chapter VII of the UN Charter to develop and enforce appropriate legal and regulatory measures against the proliferation of WMD and their means of delivery, particularly in relation to non-state actors – is certainly an area in which the GP partners could realise significant gains in combating CBRN proliferation. The GP experience to date has demonstrated that the threat posed by the proliferation of such materials and related expertise is most effectively tackled through exactly the type of co-operative and multilateral partnership which this initiative has been based on. In this respect, it makes eminent sense for the GP, as it moves to address global challenges, to ensure that its activities in the next stage are designed to enhance the values and objectives of UNSCR 1540. Those GP countries with strong legislative frameworks and the technical expertise required to help prevent CBRN proliferation are well placed to provide such support in the context of the resolution. This approach is consistent with the recommendations of the 1540 Committee's comprehensive review[25] and a Stimson Center-Stanley Foundation study on the importance of exploiting resources to meet the needs of developing states.[26] While some GP work and the EU Instrument for Stability contribute in many ways to the aims and objectives of UNSCR 1540, much more could be done under a renewed GP programme to directly support these aims and objectives should the initiative take on a global character.

---

[25] 'Final Outcome Document of 2009 Comprehensive Review: Key Findings and Recommendations', 1540 Hub, <http://1540. collaborationtools.org/node/35048>, accessed 17 June 2011.
[26] Brian Finlay and Elizabeth Turpin, 'The Next 100 Project: Leveraging National Security Assistance to Meet Developing World Needs', Conference Report, Stimson Center and Stanley Foundation, 2009, <http://www. stanleyfoundation.org/resources.cfm?ID =372>, accessed 17 June 2011.

Conclusion

There are several core challenges and issues that the extended GP multilateral threat reduction programme will need to address if the initiative is to remain relevant in line with the current and evolving global CBRN security environment. To begin with, it is important for the GP to complete all ongoing projects in Russia and the wider FSU where completion dates lie beyond 2012. Failure to do so will undermine the confidence of potential future recipients of funding with regard to the staying power of existing GP donors, and also reduce the incentive for Russia to sign up to a globalised agenda.

There is also a very strong argument for moving the GP beyond the G8 context in order to engage key countries such as China and India as donors, and to develop a framework better suited to providing a regional oversight approach to multilateral threat reduction, so long as such an approach does not limit the flexibility that the current structure offers and of course enhances the threat reduction initiatives of the biggest player, the United States. There is a possibility, of course, that moving to a more formal multilateral framework is likely to lead to more bureaucracy and duplicate what GP states themselves can offer, but this is a risk worth taking if the initiative becomes truly global in scope and membership.

Beyond organisational changes, membership and geographical expansion and project completion, the GP could clearly make a very useful contribution to encouraging a step change in work on bio-security and bio-safety issues linked to work on public health in collaboration with the WHO, FAO and OIE. In partnership with the IAEA the GP could also develop a structured and long-term programme to enhance the security of radiological materials on a global basis. The GP could also address security issues related to the chemical industry and take a more proactive role in assisting countries to meet their obligations under UNSCR 1540.

This is admittedly a broad and ambitious agenda for the GP in terms of taking the initiative forward beyond 2012. It is clear, however, that an appropriately expanded membership, an enhanced and more strategically-oriented Working Group, and a focus on addressing priority CBRN risk mitigation tasks in a truly global context could set up the GP to make a continued and invaluable contribution to the realisation of non-proliferation and CBRN security in the years ahead.

ANNEX A: GLOBAL PARTNERSHIP DOCUMENTS, KANANASKIS G8 SUMMIT, 27 JUNE 2002

Statement by G8 Leaders: The G8 Global Partnership against the Spread of Weapons and Materials of Mass Destruction

The attacks of September 11 demonstrated that terrorists are prepared to use any means to cause terror and inflict appalling casualties on innocent people. We commit ourselves to prevent terrorists, or those that harbour them, from acquiring or developing nuclear, chemical, radiological and biological weapons; missiles; and related materials, equipment and technology. We call on all countries to join us in adopting the set of non-proliferation principles we have announced today.

In a major initiative to implement those principles, we have also decided today to launch a new G8 Global Partnership against the Spread of Weapons and Materials of Mass Destruction. Under this initiative, we will support specific co-operation projects, initially in Russia, to address non-proliferation, disarmament, counter-terrorism and nuclear safety issues. Among our priority concerns are the destruction of chemical weapons, the dismantlement of decommissioned nuclear submarines, the disposition of fissile materials and the employment of former weapons scientists. We will commit to raise up to $20 billion to support such projects over the next ten years. A range of financing options, including the option of bilateral debt for program exchanges, will be available to countries that contribute to this Global Partnership. We have adopted a set of guidelines that will form the basis for the negotiation of specific agreements for new projects, that will apply with immediate effect, to ensure effective and efficient project development, co-ordination and implementation. We will review over the next year the applicability of the guidelines to existing projects.

Recognising that this Global Partnership will enhance international security and safety, we invite other countries that are prepared to adopt its common principles and guidelines to enter into discussions with us on participating in and contributing to this initiative. We will review progress on this Global Partnership at our next Summit in 2003.

* * *

The G8 Global Partnership: Principles to Prevent Terrorists, or Those that Harbour Them, from Gaining Access to Weapons or Materials of Mass Destruction

The G8 calls on all countries to join them in commitment to the following six principles to prevent terrorists or those that harbour them from acquiring or developing nuclear, chemical, radiological and biological weapons; missiles; and related materials, equipment and technology.

1. Promote the adoption, universalisation, full implementation and, where necessary, strengthening of multilateral treaties and other international instruments whose aim is to prevent the proliferation or illicit acquisition of such items; strengthen the institutions designed to implement these instruments.
2. Develop and maintain appropriate effective measures to account for and secure such items in production, use, storage and domestic and international transport; provide assistance to states lacking sufficient resources to account for and secure these items.
3. Develop and maintain appropriate effective physical protection measures applied to facilities which house such items, including defence in depth; provide assistance to states lacking sufficient resources to protect their facilities.

4. Develop and maintain effective border controls, law enforcement efforts and international co-operation to detect, deter and interdict in cases of illicit trafficking in such items, for example through installation of detection systems, training of customs and law enforcement personnel and co-operation in tracking these items; provide assistance to states lacking sufficient expertise or resources to strengthen their capacity to detect, deter and interdict in cases of illicit trafficking in these items.

5. Develop, review and maintain effective national export and transshipment controls over items on multilateral export control lists, as well as items that are not identified on such lists but which may nevertheless contribute to the development, production or use of nuclear, chemical and biological weapons and missiles, with particular consideration of end-user, catch-all and brokering aspects; provide assistance to states lacking the legal and regulatory infrastructure, implementation experience and/or resources to develop their export and transshipment control systems in this regard.

6. Adopt and strengthen efforts to manage and dispose of stocks of fissile materials designated as no longer required for defence purposes, eliminate all chemical weapons, and minimise holdings of dangerous biological pathogens and toxins, based on the recognition that the threat of terrorist acquisition is reduced as the overall quantity of such items is reduced.

* * *

The G8 Global Partnership: Guidelines for New or Expanded Co-operation Projects

The G8 will work in partnership, bilaterally and multilaterally, to develop, co-ordinate, implement and finance, according to their respective means, new or expanded co-operation projects to address (i) non-proliferation, (ii) disarmament, (iii) counter-terrorism and (iv) nuclear safety (including environmental) issues, with a view to enhancing strategic stability, consonant with our international security objectives and in support of the multilateral non-proliferation regimes. Each country has primary responsibility for implementing its non-proliferation, disarmament, counter-terrorism and nuclear safety obligations and requirements and commits its full co-operation within the Partnership.

Co-operation projects under this initiative will be decided and implemented, taking into account international obligations and domestic laws of participating partners, within appropriate bilateral and multilateral legal frameworks that should, as necessary, include the following elements:

i. Mutually agreed effective monitoring, auditing and transparency measures and procedures will be required in order to ensure that co-operative activities meet agreed objectives (including irreversibility as necessary), to confirm work performance, to account for the funds expended and to provide for adequate access for donor representatives to work sites;

ii. The projects will be implemented in an environmentally sound manner and will maintain the highest appropriate level of safety;

iii. Clearly defined milestones will be developed for each project, including the option of suspending or terminating a project if the milestones are not met;

iv. The material, equipment, technology, services and expertise provided will be solely for peaceful purposes and, unless otherwise agreed, will be used only for the purposes of implementing the projects and will not be transferred. Adequate measures of physical protection will also be applied to prevent theft or sabotage;

v. All governments will take necessary steps to ensure that the support provided will be considered free technical assistance and will be exempt from taxes, duties, levies and other charges;

vi. Procurement of goods and services will be conducted in accordance with open international practices to the extent possible, consistent with national security requirements;

vii. All governments will take necessary steps to ensure that adequate liability protections from claims related to the co-operation will be provided for donor countries and their personnel and contractors;

viii. Appropriate privileges and immunities will be provided for government donor representatives working on co-operation projects; and

ix. Measures will be put in place to ensure effective protection of sensitive information and intellectual property.

Given the breadth and scope of the activities to be undertaken, the G8 will establish an appropriate mechanism for the annual review of progress under this initiative which may include consultations regarding priorities, identification of project gaps and potential overlap, and assessment of consistency of the co-operation projects with international security obligations and objectives. Specific bilateral and multilateral project implementation will be co-ordinated subject to arrangements appropriate to that project, including existing mechanisms.

For the purposes of these guidelines, the phrase "new or expanded co-operation projects" is defined as co-operation projects that will be initiated or enhanced on the basis of this Global Partnership. All funds disbursed or released after its announcement would be included in the total of committed resources. A range of financing options, including the option of bilateral debt for program exchanges, will be available to countries that contribute to this Global Partnership.

The Global Partnership's initial geographic focus will be on projects in Russia, which maintains primary responsibility for implementing its obligations and requirements within the Partnership.

In addition, the G8 would be willing to enter into negotiations with any other recipient countries, including those of the Former Soviet Union, prepared to adopt the guidelines, for inclusion in the Partnership.

Recognising that the Global Partnership is designed to enhance international security and safety, the G8 invites others to contribute to and join in this initiative.

With respect to nuclear safety and security, the partners agreed to establish a new G8 Nuclear Safety and Security Group by the time of our next Summit.

ANNEX B: RESEARCH INTERVIEWS

Research interviews were conducted with officials from the following government departments, international organisations, project contractors and non-governmental organisations.

- Alternative Energies and Atomic Energy Commission (Commissariat à l'énergie atomique et aux énergies alternatives – CEA), France
- Bureau of International Security and Nonproliferation (ISN), US Department of State
- Crown Agents, UK
- Department of Energy and Climate Change (DECC), UK
- Department of Nuclear Safety and Security, International Atomic Energy Agency (IAEA)
- Division of Fuel Cycle and Waste Technology, Department of Nuclear Energy, IAEA
- Division of Nuclear Power (NENP), Department of Nuclear Energy, IAEA
- European Bank for Reconstruction and Development (EBRD)
- European Commission: External Relations Directorate-General (DG-RELEX)
- European Commission: European Aid Co-operation Office (AIDCO)
- Federal Foreign Office, Germany
- Foreign and Commonwealth Office, UK
- Ministry of Defence, UK
- Ministry of Foreign Affairs, Czech Republic
- Ministry of Foreign Affairs, Finland
- Ministry of Foreign Affairs, Italy
- Ministry of Foreign Affairs, Japan
- Ministry of Foreign Affairs, Norway

- Ministry of Foreign Affairs, the Netherlands
- Ministry of Foreign Affairs, Russian Federation
- Ministry of Foreign Affairs and International Trade, Canada
- National Nuclear Security Administration (NNSA), US Department of Energy
- Norwegian Radiation Protection Authority
- Nuclear Energy State Corporation (Rosatom), Russian Federation
- Nuvia Ltd, UK
- Office of Cooperative Threat Reduction, US Department of State
- Office of the Assistant Secretary of Defense for Global Strategic Affairs, US Department of Defense
- Swedish Radiation Protection Authority
- The National Academies.

ANNEX C: CASE STUDIES

This annex contains seven case studies which are presented to demonstrate the practical achievements of the Global Partnership and to highlight the work remaining to be completed. The case studies include:

- Elimination of Weapons-Grade Plutonium Production (EWGPP) programme
- Andreeva Bay – a complex nuclear legacy challenge
- Scientist redirection and engagement
- The Chernobyl Shelter project
- Securing radiological sources
- Shchuch'ye chemical weapons destruction programme
- Nuclear submarine dismantlement.

All of the information contained in the case studies has been checked for content and accuracy with those government departments or non-governmental organisations responsible for leading the related programmes described in each case study.

Case Study 1: Andreeva Bay

History
During the Cold War the Soviet Union's Northern Fleet operated some two thirds of the navy's nuclear powered vessels – submarines and icebreakers. Much of the spent nuclear fuel (SNF) and other radioactive waste (RW) from these vessels was dumped without any treatment in vastly inadequate storage at sites around the Kola Peninsula and even dumped directly into the Barents and Kara Seas. Identical approaches to the management of radioactive material took place in the far east

of Russia associated with the operation of the Russian Pacific Fleet.

The management of SNF and RW accumulated during decades of operation of the Russian nuclear fleet is one of the major challenges of the Cold War legacy in the Russian Federation. Naval SNF and RW are stored at different locations in northwest Russia and on the Pacific, with one of the main storage sites located in Andreeva Bay on the Kola Peninsula some 50 km east of the Norwegian border. About 22,000 spent fuel assemblies (SFA) equivalent to ~ 100 reactor cores are stored there in conditions that are well below current Russian and international standards and which cause gradual degradation of the fuel. When the site was an active naval facility a number of serious incidents took place, leading to radioactive contamination of buildings and groundwater.

Operations at this former naval base ceased in the 1990s and ten years later, when the base was transferred to the jurisdiction of Rosatom, all facilities and infrastructure at the site were derelict. The total assessed radioactivity of the SNF and RW stored at Andreeva Bay reaches approximately 1.5×10^{17} Becquerels – most of the activity associated with some 30 tonnes of SNF at the site. With the site becoming more hazardous each year the GP brought together expertise and funding from four GP countries to address the challenge.

Timeline
1962: Commissioning of the SNF Andreeva Bay facility for use by the Russian Northern Fleet.
1982: SNF storage tank leak leads to SNF eventually being moved to the dry storage site at this location over the next few years.
1990: Andreeva Bay abandoned by Russian Navy but SNF and other RW allegedly occasionally brought to the site for temporary storage up to the mid-1990s.
1990–2000: Gradual deterioration of the site's infrastructure and continued ground contamination of Caesium 137 and Strontium 90 from the former SNF storage building.
2000: Ministry of Atomic Energy (now Rosatom Corporation)

given responsibility for the site.

2000–01: First project involving Norway.

2001: International IAEA meeting during which the scale of the challenge facing Russia is first announced.

2002: Global Partnership launched at Kananaskis.

2003: Preliminary work implemented by UK.

2003–06: Major portfolio of UK projects undertaken in collaboration with Norway and Sweden to restore basic infrastructure to Andreeva Bay to allow safe working for eventual SNF removal.

2006–10: Major portfolio of UK projects to design and construct the infrastructure for handling SNF removal and safe working.

2014: Expected earliest date for SNF removal to commence.

Challenges

It was recognised at the end of the Cold War that without assistance Russia would lack the time, expertise, finance and infrastructure to make safe and secure its substantial inventory of hazardous nuclear material. Onshore abandoned SNF facilities such as Andreeva Bay and Gremikha were already leaking radioactive waste into the environment with increasing concern being raised by environmental groups and government nuclear safety regulators across Scandinavia. SNF was also being stored on ships moored in Murmansk harbour in far from satisfactory conditions. Recognising this challenge, some limited programmes of assistance were provided throughout the 1990s by the EU through its TACIS programme and the governments of Norway and Sweden. Although these projects identified and addressed a number of individual issues, without the co-ordinated political and financial support of a much larger international effort they were unable to address the larger challenges of making SNF safe and secure together with its eventual removal to Russia's reprocessing centre at Mayak in the Urals.

Ensuring that the SNF stored in these derelict nuclear facilities was first secured and then moved safely without presenting a risk to both the environment and those working at the sites would require larger, more expensive projects, and the necessary technical expertise to achieve it.

Solutions

Nuclear submarine dismantlement was one of the four priorities of the GP but the issue of greatest concern was not the submarines themselves, but the safety and security of the SNF either within them or stored at the former onshore bases. While the UK, Norway and Italy have funded the dismantlement of a number of submarines, their main effort, working with Sweden, Russian nuclear agencies, the European Bank for Reconstruction and Development (EBRD) and the EU TACIS programme, has focused on securing the safe and secure storage of SNF and associated radioactive waste at Andreeva Bay.

This collaborative effort is an excellent example of how the GP has enabled a significant nuclear legacy of the Cold War to be addressed using the combined technical resources of five countries, the EBRD and the EU. By working together the immense technical challenge presented by this long derelict site is now being addressed. The UK effort has focused on the design and construction of infrastructure for handling SNF and creating safe conditions for its eventual removal after 2014. Other essential infrastructure projects to support SNF removal – including building construction, site services and radioactive waste facilities – are being funded by the other international partners. UK funding also supported the construction of a long-term storage facility at Atomflot, Murmansk, for highly enriched uranium zirconium SNF from ice breakers which had been stored inappropriately on the supply ship *Lotta*.

A significant spin-off of the collaborative work at Andreeva Bay and at Atomflot has been the sharing of international expertise with Russian agencies embracing project and risk management, nuclear decommissioning and nuclear safety best practice. This should ensure Russia itself is better equipped to tackle remediation of its still sizeable inventory of hazardous legacy infrastructure.

The close multilateral co-operation with Russia to resolve a complex nuclear legacy challenge can be broken down as follows:

- The UK has led on SNF management and the associated infrastructure for its removal
- Norway is leading on site infrastructure, utilities and physical protection
- Sweden is leading on very low level radioactive waste disposal
- Italy is leading on solid and low level nuclear waste management
- Italy is leading on provision of SNF and RW transport vessels and construction of RW management complex
- The EBRD is providing funding for the handling and transport of SNF
- The EU, via TACIS, is providing canisters.

Achievements of the Collaboration at Andreeva Bay

1. The creation of an effective strategy for the safe and secure removal of the SNF
2. Establishment of good working relations between partner countries and agencies
3. A process for removing SNF which minimises the risk of nuclear incidents
4. A willingness of donors to share best practice
5. Developed a revised approach to submarine transportation with the support of Royal Navy salvage expertise
6. 1,700 m^3 of liquid radioactive waste processed
7. Achieved international environmental certification at two sites.

Case Study 2: The Chernobyl Shelter

History
On 26 April 1986 the world's worst recorded nuclear accident occurred at the Chernobyl Nuclear Power Plant in Ukraine during a test which ignored established safety measures. The accident at

number four RBMK reactor resulted in the release of large amounts of radioactive material into the atmosphere. To contain the radioactivity being released following the accident, a temporary concrete and steel shelter was put in place around the demolished reactor building. By necessity, the shelter was put together extremely quickly to constrain the release of radioactive material from the now exposed reactor core and melted uranium fuel. It was not designed as a long-term solution.

The accident resulted in international pressure on the Ukrainian government to close the Chernobyl plant because of safety concerns. In 1995 a memorandum of understanding between the G7, the EU and the government of Ukraine committed the participants to co-operate in the development of a cost effective and robust approach to convert the damaged reactor and its temporary shelter into an environmentally safe condition. A 'Chernobyl Shelter Fund' was established in 1997 at the European Bank for Reconstruction and Development (EBRD) to assist Ukraine in replacing the existing shelter over Chernobyl's destroyed Unit 4 reactor with one that would be an environmentally safe, long-life structure.

The initiative for establishing the fund was led by the G8 governments and the EU and announced at the G8 summit in Denver in 1997. Thirty countries and the European Commission have contributed to the fund since 1997 with the largest donations from G8 countries and the EU. To achieve this plan the Chernobyl Shelter Fund has financed the 'Shelter Implementation Plan' (SIP). The SIP of 1997 included US$768 million as a cost indication for the project; however, as the SIP comprised actions to be implemented in the future this was never a precise estimate. Since 1997 the estimated cost of completing the new shelter and related work has risen to some €1.54 billion. Current donations total around €860 million.

Timeline
1977: Chernobyl Unit 1 reactor commissioned and connected to the grid.
1983: Chernobyl Unit 4 reactor commissioned and connected to the grid.

1986: Chernobyl Unit 4 reactor explodes during test exercise.
1997: Chernobyl Shelter Fund established.
2004: Approval of New Safe Confinement (NSC) concept design and stabilisation work begins on the original shelter.
2007: The EBRD and Ukraine sign grant agreement for NSC.
2008: Work on constructing the NSC begins.
2015: Expected completion date for the NSC.

Challenges

Construction of the NSC is well underway and when completed it will be a freestanding, semicircular arch measuring 257m across, 105m high and 150m in length. The arch frame is a lattice construction of tubular steel members. Once the steel lattice structure is complete it will eventually be slid over the existing shelter. This is one of the biggest and most complex construction projects in Europe and involves dealing with radiological material found during the construction phase. Once completed and in place around 2015, the new structure will contain the radioactive inventory within the shelter, prevent the intrusion of rain and snow, and provide for the eventual deconstruction of the destroyed reactor and the original shelter. A further challenge to the project is funding. Significant additional funding has been provided to EBRD for the project and related work at Chernobyl since its inception in 1997, including some US$17 million provided by the Russian government in 2008. However, the final cost of constructing the NSC and associated works is now likely to be around €1.54 billion, significantly in excess of earlier estimates. With current donor contributions of some €860 million, the key challenge is to make up the shortfall at a time when national budgets are under extreme pressure because of the recession.

Solutions

The Kananaskis Summit in 2002 which saw the launch of the GP also led to the establishment of a nuclear safety and security group which took particular interest in progress to complete the shelter. While the implementation of the Chernobyl Shelter Fund in 1997 pre-dated the GP by some five years, a significant proportion of the current funds available to the EBRD have been pledged from a number of GP member states' threat reduction programmes since 2002. EBRD officials indicated during the interviews for this study that the GP was of pivotal importance to the Chernobyl Shelter because it had clearly raised the profile of international nuclear safety and security work, and helped donors to justify support for the Shelter Fund. They also highlighted the importance to the EBRD of the GP mandate being renewed beyond 2012 because another round of funding requests for the Chernobyl Shelter was inevitable given the funding shortfall in the current forecasts, let alone any future escalation of costs due to unforeseen problems in completing the NSC. Without further funding to complete the project under EBRD supervision, it would be very difficult for the Ukrainian government to find the necessary resources in an appropriate timescale given the fragility of the original shelter. The GP framework has proved to be the ideal structure to focus donor aid on multilateral projects managed by organisations such as the EBRD with the experience of delivering complex nuclear related projects.

Achievements of the EBRD's Chernobyl Project

- Implemented a complex multilateral project with unique characteristics in a difficult political and technical environment
- Shelter stabilisation measures have significantly reduced the probability of collapse of the shelter over the period that will be necessary for the construction of the NSC
- Improvements have been made to understanding the risk of criticality in Fuel Containing Masses (FCM) to the extent that this is no longer regarded as a credible event (there is now a better understanding of the requirements for the long-term monitoring of FCM)
- The management of worker and environmental safety has also improved and this is now regarded as meeting international standards.

Contributors to the Chernobyl Shelter Fund
Austria, Belgium, Canada, Denmark, the EC, Finland, France, Germany, Greece, Iceland, Ireland, Israel, Italy, Japan, Korea, Kuwait, Luxembourg, the Netherlands, Norway, Poland, Portugal, Russia, Slovak Republic, Slovenia, Spain, Sweden, Switzerland, Ukraine, the United Kingdom and the United States.

Case Study 3: Elimination of Weapons-Grade Plutonium Production (EWGPP) Programme

History
The origins of the EWGPP programme can be traced back to 1994, eight years before the creation of the GP. Despite this, the GP came to play an important, if not vital, role in the completion of the programme. The EWGPP programme evolved from a bilateral commitment made by both the US and the newly-formed Russian Federation ('Agreement between the Government of the United States of America and the Government of the Russian Federation Concerning Cooperation Regarding Plutonium Production Reactors'). It required a number of plutonium-producing reactors in the US and Russia to 'permanently cease operations', with the understanding that 'replacement sources of thermal and electrical energy should be developed'.

Timeline
1994: EWGPP agreement signed by the US and Russia.
1995: Core conversion process adopted under US Department of Defense (DoD) CTR programme.
2000: Core conversion process replaced by replacement fossil fuel power plant process.
2001: Project transferred from DoD to US Department of Energy (DoE).
2002: G8 Global Partnership created at Kananaskis.
2002–05: International donors sought.
2005: Majority of memoranda of understanding signed.
2008: Seversk reactors shut down.
2010: Zheleznogorsk reactors shut down.

Programme Structure
Included in the agreement were the Russian plutonium-producing reactors at Mayak, Seversk and Zheleznogorsk. The reactors at Seversk and Zheleznogorsk were of particular importance because they produced significant quantities of plutonium and also posed a great safety risk. With two 'closed cities' relying on the heat and electricity provided by the reactors, it was also essential that replacement energy sources were provided. Initially, it was planned that these replacements would come from reactor core conversions under the DoD CTR budget. By 2000 it became clear that financial and scheduling constraints would render this option untenable. The scope of the project subsequently switched from converting reactor cores to providing heat and power through fossil fuel power plants (FFPP). An existing FFPP at Seversk was to be refurbished and a new FFPP was to be built at Zheleznogorsk. Project responsibilities were distributed between the United States and Russia as follows: the Russian Federation was to control implementation (including, *inter alia*, design, procurement and construction), while the US would maintain contractor oversight and provide payment on verification of completed project milestones.

Challenges
With the shift in focus from reactor core replacement to FFPP replacement, the project was moved to the DoE where significant expertise in fossil fuel energy existed. From the outset of DoE oversight there was a very limited amount of congressional support for the project, and as a consequence very limited funding. The value of the US dollar was declining and material and labour costs began to rise. As a result funding priority was given to the Seversk reactors and the future of the Zheleznogosrk project was uncertain. It swiftly became clear that to provide sufficient funding to complete the Zheleznogorsk project, the US Congress would have to be assured of a certain level of international 'burden sharing'. It is here that the principles and

funding commitments created through the GP became essential to the successful completion of the EWGPP project.

Solutions

The EWGPP programme, with the assistance of the US Department of State, cultivated a number of international donors by briefing US Congressmen on the merits of the Zheleznogorsk project. Where further interest developed, Memoranda of Understanding were negotiated with each party, allowing donors to supply funds to be applied in a manner that was deemed satisfactory to both parties. By 2006, MoUs had been signed with six nations (Finland, South Korea, the Netherlands, Canada, the UK and New Zealand), providing over $30 million in external funds. The effect this had on securing congressional support is clearly seen in the funds provided. DoE funding before the provision of international funds averaged at around $60 million. By 2006 this had increased to $187 million, eventually reaching a maximum of $231 million in 2007 (nearly four times the funding given in 2002).

Memoranda of Understanding

UK: Contributed $20 million to be spent on equipment, according to an agreed schedule, and with provisions for auditing and periodic project review.

New Zealand: Contributed NZ$ 500,000 in one lump sum to be used for 'an environment-related purpose' and with provisions for auditing monthly reports.

Canada: Contributed CA$9 million to be spent in one lump sum on design work, with provisions for auditing, monthly reports and public communication of contribution.

Achievements of the Zheleznogorsk Project

- Closure prevented more than 1.2 metric tonnes of weapons-grade plutonium being produced annually
- Focused funding on a key priority of the GP

- A model example of burden sharing and as such convinced Congress to approve the remaining funding
- An excellent example of 'piggybacking' which enabled new GP contributions to a project to be made via extant arrangements, thus saving time and money in negotiating new contracts and agreements to disburse funding.

Case Study 4: Securing Radiological Sources

History
Across the globe millions of radioactive sources are used every day for medical, industrial, research and commercial purposes, all of which need to be adequately secured both during and after their economic usefulness. While safe handling and security of radiological sources is required to protect the public and those using them, one type of threat that is of particular concern is the potential for terrorist attacks with radiological dispersal devices (RDDs). Such weapons are designed to spread radiological particles over a large area using explosive or other means, thus causing substantial panic and disruption to the communities targeted. Of the millions of sources used worldwide only a small proportion are powerful enough to cause serious harm but include americium-241, californium-252, caesium-137, colbalt-60, iridium-192, plutonium-238 and strontium-90. One of the main difficulties in ensuring all radiological sources are adequately protected is that many thousands have been lost, abandoned, stolen or just not registered under government licensing systems, where such systems exist. Sources outside the control and protection of government regulations or licensing are known as 'orphan sources'. The IAEA has no estimate of the number of orphan sources yet to be recovered and secured. There has never been a global inventory of radiological sources, although the IAEA recognises the value of national registers.

After 9/11 the IAEA drew up an expanded programme to improve the security of nuclear and other radioactive material, subject to voluntary funding and resources being made available by member states to the agency's Nuclear Security Fund (NSF).

A key focus of the IAEA Nuclear Security Plan is securing orphan sources and the agency's work in this area provides an example of the scale of the challenge. The IAEA was directly involved in improving the security of nearly 4,800 individual radioactive sources in more than thirty-five countries between January 2002 and December 2009.

Timeline
1970s: IAEA training in nuclear security started.
1975: First recommendations issued for the Physical Protection of Nuclear Materials.
2002: GP launched at Kananaskis.
2002: Inception of the Nuclear Security Fund as part of the IAEA's first Nuclear Security Plan 2002–05.
2006: Nuclear Security Plan 2006–09 agreed.
September 2009: IAEA Nuclear Security Plan 2010–13 agreed.
April 2010: Nuclear Security Summit.

Challenges
Although President's Obama's Nuclear Security Summit in April 2010 had its prime focus on fissile material, the summit *communiqué* 'recognised that measures contributing to nuclear material security have value in relation to the security of radio-active substances and encourage efforts to secure those materials as well'. A number of states – Belgium, Norway, New Zealand and the UK – pledged additional contributions to the NSF, some of which were earmarked to secure orphan sources and some were derived from GP budgets. Even with these voluntary additions of financial resources, the funding available to the IAEA for tackling even the Cold War legacy in orphan sources in the FSU is well below that required to address the challenge in a desirable timescale. Keeping track of radioactive sources in use and locating orphan sources in developing countries will potentially be even more difficult than in the FSU countries.

The difficulty in detecting radioactive sources presents a further challenge in preventing radiological terrorism. Many sources are comparatively small and effective detection, when attempts are made to smuggle such materials across borders and checkpoints, depends on vigilant and trained border guards and adequately maintained detection equipment. While such 'second line of defence measures' are vital in preventing radiological material from getting into the hands of terrorist groups, locating and securing all such material in a country in compliance with the IAEA's Code of Conduct on the Safety and Security of Radioactive Sources would be the preferred approach for sustainable, long-term security.

Solutions

The security of radiological materials was not one of the four GP priorities in 2002, and it attracted second billing in the April 2010 Nuclear Security Summit *communiqué*. This is somewhat perverse given the importance many countries and the IAEA now attach to the challenge of locating and securing orphan sources, given their potential to be used in a RDD. The NSF, overseen and managed by the IAEA's Office of Nuclear Security, and the Global Threat Reduction Initiative programme of the US National Nuclear Security Administration, both offer excellent routes for GP-funded work on nuclear security. Both the NSF and NNSA programmes offer existing legal frameworks and technical expertise in a broad range of nuclear security matters particularly related to the physical protection of facilities and training for security personnel designed to strengthen security procedure and culture. Fast-tracking of future projects on both securing orphan sources and enhancing border controls (in terms of equipment, training and best practice) using the significant funding sources offered through the GP framework would enable GP countries to widen the geographical scope of their threat reduction programmes much more quickly than would be the case without these existing programmes.

Achievements of the IAEA Nuclear Security Programme

- Provided an effective instrument for GP countries, the EU and other donors to contribute to the securing of orphan sources – some 4,800 up to the end of 2009
- Provision of independent nuclear security best practice advice to states

- Physical protection upgrades conducted in over one hundred sites in more than thirty-five countries
- More than 3,000 detection instruments supplied to fifty-five states.

Contributors to the IAEA NSF
Thirty countries, the EU, the Nuclear Threat Initiative and the United Nations Interregional Crime Research Institute have contributed some $116 million to the NSF over the period 2002–09. A further ~$10 million was pledged at the Nuclear Security Summit in April 2010.

Case Study 5: Scientist Redirection and Engagement

History
A decade after the end of the Cold War Russia's nuclear weapons complex, embracing ten closed cities from Sarov in the west to Zheleznogorsk in eastern Siberia, still housed some 760,000 inhabitants and employed approximately 124,000 workers, of whom around 10–15 per cent were specialists with proliferation sensitive knowledge, and a further 20–30 per cent with access to radiological materials. In addition, at least 3,000 nuclear specialists possessed proliferation-sensitive knowledge in other countries of the former Soviet Union (FSU). Many more support personnel also had knowledge of, and access to, radiological materials which could be of value to a proliferating state or terrorist organisation. During the Cold War, the Soviet Union also supported a massive biological warfare (BW) programme employing tens of thousands of specialists across over forty research facilities. In 1992, then Russian President Boris Yeltsin issued a decree prohibiting any further offensive BW activities, but many of the specialists and institutes working on these biological programmes were not disbanded and redirected their efforts to non-weapons biological research.

The end of the Cold War and the dismantling of the FSU's administrative structures brought the Soviet Union's research and development activities in the CBRN field to an abrupt halt. Researchers in this field saw their standards of living plummet and the opportunities to use their know-how shrink. There was a real danger in the early 1990s of a mass exodus by former Soviet scientists to countries interested in acquiring such expertise to fast-track their own programmes, and to terrorist groups wishing to use CBRN materials for malevolent purposes. A further concern of the international community was the continued risks posed by dual-use knowledge, particularly related to biological science, given the potential to move from 'public good' research to the development of a CBRN weapons capability. This latter concern has now considerably widened with the global growth of the biotechnology industry embracing both human health and the agricultural industry.

Criteria for Successful Scientist Engagement

General:

- Assist scientific institutes in securing stable funding from diverse sources and provide a secure career path for personnel
- Educate all personnel to adopt a culture of 'professional responsibility' embracing safety, safeguards and security
- Collaborate in developing knowledge and sharing lessons learned of safely using technologies and managing risk
- Encourage long-term international scientific and technological collaboration, including fostering scientist exchange with trusted partner countries and international scientific networks.

Specific to nuclear:

- Comply with IAEA guidelines relating to nuclear security, safety and safeguards.

Specific to bio:

- Comply with World Health Organization guidelines for bio-security and bio-safety.

Challenges

It was recognised at the end of the Cold War that without assistance FSU countries would not have the resources to redirect the talents of their former weapons scientists to peaceful purposes in a meaningful timescale. In recognition of this, individual programmes of assistance were established throughout the 1990s by the US Cooperative Threat Reduction (CTR) programme. A key international initiative supported by the European Commission, the US and Japan was the establishment of two centres to prevent the proliferation of CBRN expertise through science and technology collaboration. These two centres – the International Science and Technology Center (ISTC) in Moscow, and the Science and Technology Center Ukraine (STCU) in Kiev – have been operating since 1994. Some 90,000 scientists and their team members were involved in the research projects supported by the centres over the period 1994 to 2008, embracing around 4,000 projects valued at nearly US$1 billion. Despite all this international support for scientist redirection since the 1990s in the FSU, it has been very difficult to measure the effectiveness of the assistance, especially the long-term sustainability of new commercial opportunities spun off from the R&D supported by these programmes. Similarly, ensuring scientists with dual-use expertise outside the FSU secure their expertise from misuse and follow international standards of professional responsibility is now recognised as one of the main proliferation challenges. This is becoming increasingly urgent as some fifty countries have expressed interest in developing a nuclear power capability, the biotechnology industry expands, and dual-use expertise becomes more widely available, requiring increased national oversight and control.

Solutions

The inclusion of scientist redirection as one of the top four priorities of the GP in 2002 successfully motivated the initiation of additional support for scientist redirection work with a specific focus by the UK on creating new, lasting non-weapons employment opportunities for former weapons scientists and technicians. Earlier US programmes, while seeking to exploit commercial opportunities, also paid as much attention to keeping scientists gainfully employed and occupied with grant-aided research at their institutes. This was undertaken to build a relationship of trust with the various institutes supported via engagement and the establishment of good working relations between Russian and American agencies.

While France and Canada have supported redirection activities, the UK programme implemented the largest of the new programmes after 2002, both in terms of breadth and impact. The UK programme has supported projects in Russia, Ukraine, Kazakhstan, Armenia, Georgia and Belarus with an emphasis on enhancing the economic well being of the targeted communities through a portfolio of instruments (investment grants for new businesses, human resource development and training, local economic development and partnership building). This holistic approach to redirection and engagement is forecast to have created some 3,000 sustainable jobs by 2012.

A number of GP countries and the European Union, through its Instrument for Stability programme, are increasing their efforts to address concerns over dual-use expertise in the biotechnology area and to enhance bio-safety and bio-security globally. Making use of the public health and agricultural benefits of future (dual-use) biological science should enable projects to be sustainable and enhance professional responsibility.

Achievements of the UK Programme

- On target to have created some 3,000 sustainable jobs by 2012
- A substantial body of 'lessons learned' experience to assist the further economic regeneration of the closed cities
- Organisational capacity built and skills transferred to permit continued job creation in the future
- Russian agencies understand and support the jobs creation and engagement effort.

Case Study 6: Shchuch'ye Chemical Weapons Destruction

History

Although the destruction of Russia's stockpile of chemical weapons (CW) is one of the four main pillars of the GP, it was an area of great concern ten years prior to its creation. Thawing relations between the US and Russia allowed the creation of the Bilateral Destruction Agreement (a chemical weapons limitation agreement) in 1992 which was bolstered over the next decade by funds from the US CTR programme, and eventually subsumed by the Chemical Weapons Convention (CWC) of 1997. The CWC set a number of stockpile destruction milestones for states parties to meet and for Russia, which declared a massive stockpile of 40,000 tonnes, meeting these milestones was always going to be a challenge without international assistance. Out of several planned or operational chemical weapons destruction (CWD) facilities in Russia, the US CTR programme chose to assist in the construction of a destruction facility near the CW stockpiles at Shchuch'ye in the Urals. This site was of particular concern not just because of the quantity of CW stored there (approximately 1.9 million munitions; some 14 per cent of Russian stockpiles), but also because of the nature of the CW; many small, lethal, proliferation-sensitive nerve gas munitions were stored in poorly secured conditions.

Timeline

1992: Joint US-Russian implementation agreement.

1996: US contracts awarded for the design and construction of the Shchuch'ye facility.

1997: Chemical Weapons Convention enters into force.

2001: National Defense Authorization Act for 2002.

2002: Global Partnership created at Kananaskis.

2003: Construction of supporting infrastructure begins at Shchuch'ye.

2007: Russia meets CWC milestone of 20 per cent of stockpile destroyed.

2009: Construction of supporting infrastructure completed; operations start in first destruction building in March.

December 2009: Russia meets CWC milestone of 45 per cent of stockpile destroyed.

Programme Structure
Throughout the Shchuch'ye project, a division of labour was maintained between the US and Russia. The US assumed responsibility for the planning, design and construction of most of the main destruction facility, while Russia assumed responsibility for one of the two destruction operation buildings, and the entire supporting infrastructure outside the perimeter fence. This included electrical and water supplies, communications, logistics and security facilities. By 2002 the US had spent over $200 million on the Shchuch'ye project, while Russian progress at this and other facilities had been slow. Recognising this, the US Congress placed certain requirements that had to be fulfilled before further US funds could be released. The 2002 National Defense Authorization Act (NDAA), passed by Congress only six months before the creation of the GP, required, amongst other things, a $25 million annual commitment by the Russians, and a 'demonstrated commitment from the international community to fund and build infrastructure needed to support and operate the facility'. Before the GP was even created, then, the programme structure of the Shchuch'ye facility created an explicit role for the international community: while the US builds the main destruction facility, Russia, with assistance from the international community, builds the supporting infrastructure.

Challenges
Large numbers of small, diverse projects (like those which make up the supporting infrastructure of a CWD facility) present many potential problems for the type of effective and co-ordinated action required by the CWC and the US NDAA – delays and costs caused by establishing numerous legal agreements and co-ordinating bureaucracies between a large number of international donors can at a minimum cause the late delivery of project goals, and at worst discourage the provision of support to begin with. Within the ten years that had passed between the initial implementation agreement between the US and Russia and

the creation of the GP, only one CWD facility had become operational in Russia. Funding, designing and contractual issues had slowed progress in Russia and, without a high-level co-ordinating mechanism, similar problems would have been encountered in the mobilisation of international support. With the creation of the GP the international community was not only given the political go-ahead to support the Shchuch'ye project, but also a unique co-ordination mechanism which allowed a large number of donors to provide support which was utilised in a timely, efficient and effective manner.

Solutions

Many of the financial commitments made by GP members to Shchuch'ye were made possible by 'piggybacking' arrangements. Instead of each potential donor securing their own legal agreements with Russia, the UK acted as a lead donor, having created a single legal agreement which could channel the assistance of other states. Contributing states were then able to donate to the UK programme through their own bilateral memoranda of understanding, ensuring that their contribution would go directly to agreed projects. Donating states received full reports on the expenditure of their contributions, and in many cases were able to visit project sites. This allowed states to contribute what they could, when they could, to projects which reflected their own interests. This mechanism became so successful that twelve states and one non-governmental organisation contributed over $90 million through the assistance programme managed by the UK. Importantly, the majority of these contributing states are not members of the G8. Although not bound by GP commitments, smaller states were able to contribute to international security in ways that may not have been financially and politically possible without the GP.

Examples of Projects

- Water supply – first completed project, funded by a $2.2 million contribution from the UK

- Railway – rail system built to transport munitions from storage to destruction facilities. Funded by $15 million contribution from Canada and $1 million contribution from the Nuclear Threat Initiative (NTI)
- Electrical supply – substations and power lines to provide and regulate electrical power. Funded by contributions from the UK, Norway, the EU, New Zealand, the Czech Republic, Sweden, the Netherlands, Belgium, Finland and Ireland totalling $8.3 million
- Destruction equipment procurement – procurement of equipment for one of the two destruction operation buildings supported by contributions from ten states totalling over $47 million.

Achievements

- Completion of infrastructure projects led by the UK has enabled the Shchuch'ye facility to become operational and enabled Russia to meet a CWC Treaty deadline (45 per cent at December 2009)
- An excellent example of piggybacking which enabled substantial GP contributions to projects to be made on a co-ordinated basis via extant arrangements, thus saving time and money in negotiating new contracts and agreements to disburse funding
- An excellent example of international collaboration where a number of GP countries have worked successfully together to complete a major CWD facility.

Case Study 7: Submarine Dismantling

History

By the turn of the century the Soviet fleet of over 200 nuclear submarines had been reduced to a Russian fleet of only forty-five, with half of these stationed on the northwest coast and the other half on the Pacific coast. However, the decommissioned submarines had not disappeared and in military shipyards, docks and moorings in northwest Russia and the Russian far east, many of the submarines remained, exposed to the elements and awaiting dismantlement. Without the required financial resources, forward planning and infrastructure Russia could not effectively dismantle all of these submarines which threatened to become a disastrous nuclear safety hazard. In addition, the highly radioactive reactor compartments, radioactive waste and SNF contained within deteriorating hulls could eventually cause substantial damage to the surrounding environment. Ensuring that the slow, hazardous and expensive task of dismantling these submarines was undertaken safely and securely was not just a concern for Russia alone, but rather a concern for the international community as a whole and especially for Russia's neighbours, with some like Norway just a few kilometres from the submarines' location. With only an estimated fifteen years before these submarines would deteriorate, some to a catastrophic degree, the GP brought together funding from seventeen states, the expertise of the IAEA Contact Expert Group (CEG) and the collaboration of military organisations from four states to launch the most extensive network of co-ordinated assistance projects carried out under the initiative.

Dismantling a Nuclear Submarine

The nuclear submarines awaiting dismantlement in Russia are up to 175 m in length and can displace up to 48,000 tonnes of water when submerged. Dismantling such a complicated vessel involves a number of steps and facilities. It has been estimated that the entire process can cost between $8 million and $10 million.

1. The submarine is carefully moved from its mooring to a shipyard, ensuring that no further damage is done to the already weak hull
2. The spent nuclear fuel and radioactive waste is removed and transferred to interim storage facilities, before eventually being transferred to long-term storage

3. The de-fuelled submarine is moved to a dry dock or slipway, where dismantlement can begin
4. The submarine is divided into three sections, with one section containing the highly radioactive reactor and its surrounding components
5. The reactor section is moved to a long-term storage facility where, over some hundred years, the latent radiation can slowly decay
6. The remaining two sections are carefully stripped of all recyclable components and eventually fully dismantled.

Challenges

It was recognised at the end of the Cold War that without assistance Russia would lack the time, expertise, finance and infrastructure to dismantle its fleet in a timely, safe and secure manner. Onshore abandoned spent nuclear fuel facilities such as Andreeva Bay and Gremikha near the border with Norway were already leaking waste into the environment, while on the Pacific coast radioactive waste was simply being dumped into the Sea of Japan. In recognition of this, individual programmes of assistance were provided throughout the 1990s by the US CTR programme, Norway, Japan and the EU. Although these projects identified and addressed a number of individual issues such as the lack of equipment and SNF transportation, without the co-ordinated political and financial support of a much larger international effort they were unable to address the larger, more holistic issues. Shipyard facilities were in poor condition, workers were badly paid and untrained in rigorous environmental protection and nuclear safety procedures. Ensuring that decommissioned submarines were dismantled to schedule without sacrificing environmental and nuclear safety would require larger, more expensive projects. These projects would have to build on existing facilities and expertise to bring them up to a fully operational standard without sacrificing stringent environmental control.

Solutions

The inclusion of nuclear submarine dismantlement as one of the top four priorities of the GP successfully motivated the support of a large number of nations for addressing this issue. The largest of these programmes, initiated by Canada, demonstrates well the holistic approach facilitated by the GP. Three separate projects, amounting to a total donation of CA$215 million, were implemented to address nearly every stage of dismantlement. Acting initially as a donor to programmes managed by others, Canada accumulated expertise and best practices through collaboration with the IAEA Contact Expert Group (CEG), the Arctic Military Environmental Collaboration (AMEC) and the European Bank for Reconstruction and Development (EBRD) until it was able to manage projects directly with Russia. After donating to the EBRD project in northwest Russia, Canada went on to initiate two bilateral programmes with Russia. The first of these in northwest Russia committed CA$120 million to the dismantlement of twelve submarines and the provision of infrastructure projects including nuclear and radiological safety training for shipyard managers. The second project provided CA$80 million for the de-fuelling and dismantlement of six further submarines and the completion of five infrastructure projects in eastern Russia, including further nuclear and radiological safety training and an upgrade to local SNF transportation. It is worth noting that these projects did not replace existing expertise and infrastructure; instead, the projects enhanced it to a level where Russia could safely and efficiently dismantle the rest of its remaining nuclear submarines. This approach reduced dangerous leakages by 30 per cent, reduced project management costs to less than 5 per cent of the total donation, and allowed the sharing of best practices with collaborating states including the UK, US and France.

Achievements of the Canadian Programme

- De-fuelling of eighteen nuclear powered submarines with fifteen fully dismantled
- Twenty-nine infrastructure projects completed
- Developed a revised approach to submarine transportation with the support of the Royal Navy
- 1,700 m^3 of liquid radioactive waste processed

- Achieved international environmental certification at two sites.

Wider Benefits of the GP Submarine Dismantlement Programmes

- UK involvement in dismantling four Russian submarines has provided invaluable information for planning the dismantlement of twenty-seven of the UK's own nuclear submarines, none of which have been dismantled yet
- Enhanced collaboration on a wide range of nuclear safety issues across the former Soviet Union
- Encouraged international environmental and nuclear safety standards to be adopted in Russia.

ANNEX D: EU INSTRUMENT FOR STABILITY

The EU Security Strategy adopted by the European Council in December 2003 identified the key threats as terrorism, the proliferation of weapons of mass destruction, regional conflicts, state failure and organised crime. In its conclusions of November 2004,[1] the European Council subsequently recognised the importance of taking into account the links between security and development for the effectiveness of the EU external action. The Instrument for Stability (IfS)[2] was later created in 2006, as part of the reform of the EU's external financing instruments to provide the EU with a strategic tool to address a number of global security challenges that are, in addition to sources of insecurity for states and their citizens, in many instances impediments to development.

Priority 1 actions in the area of risk mitigation and preparedness relate to CBRN materials or agents as well as associated knowledge. Some €266 million of the Instrument for Stability's budget for 2007–13 has been dedicated to the non-proliferation of CBRN weapons. These actions now form one of the key means of supporting the European Security Strategy.[3] A number of countries both within and outside the EU, as well as

---

[1] 'Presidency Conclusions', European Council, Brussels, 4–5 November 2004, <http://www.consilium.europa.eu/uedocs/cms_data/docs/pressdata/en/ec/82534.pdf>, accessed 17 June 2011.

[2] Regulation (EC) No 1717/2006 of the European Parliament and the Council, 15 November 2006, establishing an Instrument for Stability, *Official Journal of the European Union* L 327/1, 24 November 2006.

[3] 'A Secure Europe in a Better World: European Security Strategy', Brussels, 12 December 2003, p. 14, <http://www.consilium.europa.eu/uedocs/cmsUpload/78367.pdf>, accessed 17 June 2011.

international and intergovernmental agencies and non-governmental actors, are implementing or financially supporting programmes which are effectively complementary to the IfS. These Priority 1 actions therefore contribute to wider international security and risk mitigation initiatives such as the GP, UNSCR 1540,[4] the Global Initiative to Combat Nuclear Terrorism (GICNT) and the global regimes (notably the NPT, CWC and BWC) and other initiatives designed to combat CBRN proliferation to non-state actors.

---

[4] 'Security Council Decides All States Shall Act to Prevent the Proliferation of Mass Destruction Weapons: Resolution 1540 (2004), Adopted Unanimously, Focuses Attention on Non-State Actors', Press Release 8076, UN Security Council, Security Council, 4956th Meeting (PM), 28 April 2004, <http://www.un.org/News/Press/docs/2004/sc8076.doc.htm>, accessed 17 June 2011.

ANNEX E: US THREAT REDUCTION PROGRAMMES

The US threat reduction programmes[1] focus around three government departments: Defense, Energy and State, with the State Department leading on GP policy matters. Between 2002 and September 2009, these programmes have committed some $10 billion to a substantial global portfolio of CBRN threat reduction work.

US Department of Energy

The US Department of Energy supports a comprehensive portfolio of threat reduction activities through its National Nuclear Security Administration (NNSA). Key programmes include:

- The Global Threat Reduction Initiative (GTRI),[2] whose projects reduce and protect vulnerable nuclear and radiological materials located at civilian sites worldwide. The current GTRI programme has involved the recovery of orphan radiological sources and the development of LEU fuel to allow conversion of Russian and Russian-supplied research reactors using HEU fuel

---

[1] Details of these programmes are set out in the Global Partnership annual report. See 'Global Partnership Annual Report', <http://www.canadainternational.gc.ca/g8/assets/pdfs/FINAL%20-%20GPWG%20Report%202010%20-%20Annex%20A%20-%20June%2017%20_2_.pdf>, accessed 17 June 2011.

[2] See 'Fact Sheet: GTRI: Reducing Nuclear Threats', NNSA, US Department of Energy, <http://nnsa.energy.gov/mediaroom/factsheets/reducingthreats>, accessed 17 June 2011.

- International Material Protection and Cooperation: Second Line of Defense.[3] Projects here include risk and vulnerability assessments of nuclear facilities; the installation of modern equipment to correct vulnerabilities; training and equipment to support installed upgrades and installation of radiation detection equipment to detect illicit smuggling of nuclear and radiological materials
- The Nonproliferation and International Security[4] programme covers a wide range of non-proliferation and security-related initiatives. Projects include work on export control to improve licensing regimes for dual-use goods, scientist redirection, warhead dismantlement and civil nuclear power reactor security upgrades. The programme also embraces responsibility for the Elimination of Weapons-Grade Plutonium Production (EWGPP),[5] Plutonium Disposition, the International Nuclear Cooperation Programme (INCP) – the co-operative effort to improve the safety at Soviet-designed nuclear power plants – and the monitoring of the conversion of 500 metric tonnes of Russian HEU from dismantled nuclear weapons to LEU for use in US nuclear power reactors.

Department of Defense (DoD)

The Cooperative Threat Reduction programmes of the DoD[6] encompass a comprehensive portfolio of CBRN threat

---

[3] See 'Fact Sheet: NNSA's Second Line of Defense Program', NNSA, US Department of Energy, <http://nnsa.energy.gov/mediaroom/factsheets/nnsassecondlineofdefenseprogram>, accessed 17 June 2011.

[4] See 'Nonproliferation Brochure', NNSA, US Department of Energy, <http://nnsa.energy.gov/sites/default/files/nnsa/inlinefiles/DNN_Nonproliferation_Brochure_0710.pdf>, accessed 17 June 2011.

[5] See case study on EWGPP.

[6] For a detailed description of these programmes see Amy F Woolf, *Nonproliferation and Threat Reduction Assistance: US Programs in the Former Soviet Union*, CRS Report to Congress, Congressional Research Service, 4 February 2010, <http://www.fas.org/sgp/crs/nuke/RL31957.pdf>, accessed 17 June 2011.

reduction projects, including strategic nuclear arms elimination, enhancement of security, safety and control of weapons in storage, biological threat reduction initiatives to consolidate and secure dangerous pathogen collections, construction of the chemical weapons destruction facility at Shchuch'ye and projects to detect the illicit trafficking of WMD materials.

The DoD also manages the International Counter-Proliferation Program (ICP) which was created by Congress in 1995 to counter the spread of weapons of mass destruction, materials and components across borders and through the territories of participating countries. It is an interagency programme consisting of subject matter expert instructors and course materials drawn from the DoD, the Federal Bureau of Investigation (FBI) and Department for Homeland Security (DHS).

Department of State and Other Agencies

The Department of State's threat reduction activities[7] encompass a comprehensive portfolio of projects focused on export control and related border security assistance across the globe, and in particular for FSU countries; a range of scientist redirection and engagement initiatives embracing CBRN facilities globally, as well as funding for the science centres in Moscow and Kiev; and the Preventing Nuclear Smuggling Program (PNSP), which seeks to address critical gaps in the capabilities of partner countries to combat the smuggling of nuclear and radiological materials.

The State Department is also responsible for the Nonproliferation and Disarmament Fund (NDF).[8] Established in 1994, the NDF allows the US to rapidly respond to unanticipated or unusually difficult, high priority non-proliferation and disarmament opportunities, circumstances or conditions.

---

[7] See Office of Cooperative Threat Reduction (ISN/CTR), State Department, <http://www.state.gov/t/isn/58381.htm>, accessed 17 June 2011.

[8] See 'Nonproliferation and Disarmament Fund', <http://www.state.gov/t/isn/ndf/>, accessed 17 June 2011.

The Nuclear Regulatory Commission[9] provides support to nuclear safety and security regulators in the FSU for a range of projects to enhance nuclear safety and security at civil nuclear power plants, and to regulators to implement key provisions of the IAEA Code of Conduct on the Safety and Security of Radioactive Sources.

The US Agency for International Development (USAID)[10] provides the US contributions to the Chernobyl Shelter project managed by the EBRD.

---

[9] See US Nuclear Regulatory Commission, <http://www.nrc.gov/>, accessed 17 June 2011.

[10] See US Agency for International Development, <http://www.usaid.gov/>, accessed 17 June 2011.

ANNEX F: NON-G8 GP COUNTRY COMMITMENTS AND EXPENDITURE

Country	Commitment/Expenditure US$ millions 2002 to April 2010
Australia	10.1
Belgium	11.3
Czech Republic	3.1
Denmark	25.2
Finland	34.1
Ireland	4.9
Netherlands	47.4
New Zealand	3.6
Norway	136.0
Poland	0.1
Republic of South Korea	3.7
Sweden	~80.0*
Ukraine	0.8
Switzerland	15.3
Total	**~US$376 million**

*Includes €16 million contributed to the EBRD's Northern Dimension Partnership Fund, some of which is spent on environmental projects in Russia.

Notes: The annual returns on expenditure and commitments for GP countries are not in a standard format and are in a range of currencies. For some countries the way the project information is presented means it is not always possible to calculate precise expenditure and commitment totals. This is particularly the case for the returns from Sweden. Commitments are also in many cases spread over a number of years as well as on different financial year periods. The above figures should therefore be seen as approximate.

Source: The financial data in this table is derived from the Global Partnership Working Group Annual Reports, 2004–10.

www.ingramcontent.com/pod-product-compliance
Ingram Content Group UK Ltd.
Pitfield, Milton Keynes, MK11 3LW, UK
UKHW020348010325
455677UK00021B/354